Handbook of Instructional Resources and References for Teaching the Gifted

Second Edition

Handbook of Instructional Resources and References for Teaching the Gifted

Frances A. Karnes
University of Southern Mississippi

Emily C. Collins
Newton, Mississippi

ALLYN AND BACON, INC.
Boston London Sydney Toronto

Library of Congress Cataloging in Publication Data

Karnes, Frances A.
  Handbook of instructional resources and references for teaching the gifted.

  Bibliography: p.
  1. Gifted children—Education—Bibliography.
2. Teaching—Aids and devices—Bibliography. 3. Gifted children—Education. 4. Teaching—Aids and devices.
I. Collins, Emily C. II. Title.
Z5814.G5K37 1984 [LC3993]   016.37195   83-22366
ISBN 0-205-08151-7

Printed in the United States of America

10 9 8 7 6 5 4 3 2   89 88 87 86 85 84

Contents

Tables

Preface

The excellent response to the first edition, as well as the number of new publications of materials and references, clearly indicated the need for a revision of the *Handbook*. Many helpful suggestions have been received from reviewers, teachers, and other professional colleagues. Some were incorporated, while others were beyond the scope and purpose of this book.

Those suggested changes that were made, however, included expanding the materials listing to encompass items appropriate for students at the secondary level, and adding information on leadership. The materials section has been expanded further with listings of new books and educational materials, as has the professional references section. Books pertinent to the utilization of computers have been added to the latter. Some deletions were made in the materials listing when the item was no longer available or the publisher could not be located after diligent search.

Several reviewers expressed the desire that more detailed materials reviews be provided. Specifically, it was proposed that we present a cost-effectiveness rating of each material and that a qualitative rating, allowing for comparability of individual items, be given as well. A major premise of this book, however, is that meeting individual student needs and individual program goals and objectives should be the chief consideration in materials selection. Individual student needs and program goals and objectives are likely to be quite diverse. We feel, therefore, that it would be impossible to give quality and cost-effectiveness ratings that would be appropriate for all programs. To do so would also be antithetical to the purposes of the handbook. Professional judgment at the program level must be utilized in the selection process and should not be undermined by author ratings.

An additional suggestion was in the area of computer science. In the final chapter information on computer utilization for gifted students is delineated. The rationale for the use of computers in the educational process, suggestions and cautions in software selection, and current and future needs and trends are detailed. Listing specific software programs appropriate for gifted students is beyond the scope of this book. The sheer numerousness of software programs precludes such a listing.

The main purpose of the second edition, like that of the first, is to design a guide for selecting commercially produced materials that are appropriate for gifted students, as well as to supply professional references pertinent to the education of the gifted. The handbook is specifically designed for educators, but it should also interest parents, college and university students enrolled in education courses, as well as anyone concerned with the education of the gifted.

Our aim is twofold: (1) to provide a central listing of currently available commercially produced materials that have been suggested as appropriate for the gifted, and that are consistent with their educational needs in the various curriculum areas as well as in creativity, logical and critical thinking, values clarification, group dynamics, and futurism; and (2) to provide an objective annotated bibliography of professional books on gifted and talented students, creativity, values clarification, logical thinking, leadership, and computers, and other books pertinent to the education of the gifted.

The vast number of publishers, distributors, and currently available commercial materials has made oversights probable, but certainly not intentional. Professionals in the field may recognize the deletion of some materials included in the first edition of this book. This is primarily because several publishers could not be located after many efforts.

There is such diversity of specialized interests that some materials and resources are beyond the scope of this book. Those materials and resources that are appropriate for the development of particular talents and gifts in the arts, music, theater, and related areas are not included. For reasons of space and scope of this book, the many excellent handbooks, resources, and references produced by state and local education agencies have been omitted; these free or inexpensive resources may be obtained by contacting state department of education consultants on gifted students. Materials are included that allow teachers to expand curriculum; therefore, basal texts and series are omitted.

Our intent is not to advertise specific materials or references, merely to list suggested items, and supply readers with the broadest listing possible. All reasonable care was taken to insure the accuracy of the information; however, prices, addresses, and publications are subject to change without notice. Lastly, while commercially prepared materials can be effectively used in educational programming for gifted students, the ultimate success of the program lies with the teachers, administrators, and parents.

ACKNOWLEDGMENTS

The road to the completion of this manuscript has been lined with many persons who willingly and generously contributed their time, energy, and concepts to expand and enhance the differentiated educational opportunities of the gifted/talented at the elementary and secondary school levels. Unfortunately, the number of these people is so vast that it is impossible to cite each by name.

In searching for appropriate materials and references for gifted students, professionals, and parents, we were fortunate to receive complimentary and examination copies from manufacturers, publishers, and distributors who were most generous in supplying them. Publisher representatives in Mississippi and the Southeast have been particularly interested in and supportive of our endeavors.

Students enrolled in classes in gifted education at the University of Southern Mississippi have offered suggestions for materials and given advice on the evaluation. Teachers, consultants, program directors, state supervisors, teacher educators, and other professional colleagues from across the nation have willingly contributed their ideas on materials and references. Teachers in the resource rooms for the gifted in the Mississippi public schools have contributed great insight into materials selection.

Special words of thanks are extended to Dr. James E. Whorton, chairman of the Special Education Department at the University of Southern Mississippi. Our gratitude is also given to our other colleagues in the department and throughout the university for their inspiration and support.

Our appreciation and gratitude will always be given to our husbands, Dr. M. Ray Karnes and Dr. Tom Collins, for their assistance in various aspects of the development of the manuscript, but most of all for their endless encouragement and patience. Our parents have also provided their unceasing support for our endeavors. Our thanks also go to Christopher and John, to the gifted students who have participated in the Center for Gifted Students at the University of Southern Mississippi; and to the gifted students in the Newton public schools, who have given true meaning to differentiated education.

INTRODUCTORY REMARKS

Recent years have brought about a heightened consciousness of the need for educational programs that are tailored to meet the unique needs of each individual student. This has fostered a renewed awareness of the necessity of specialized educational programming for the gifted. Increasing commitment to meeting the educational needs of the gifted is evidenced in the growing number of specialized programs for gifted students within the public schools. General educators, administrators, and counselors are also voicing concern for adapting the general curriculum in order to meet more effectively the instructional needs of the gifted. State departments of education have extended their leadership roles by substantially increasing the number of full-time state coordinators of gifted programs. Many colleges and universities are offering courses in the education of the gifted in response to the growing need for trained personnel. The concern of parents, educators, and other interested citizens has led to the enactment of state and federal legislation pertaining to educational provisions for gifted students within the public schools. It is hoped that this compilation of materials and resources will assist all those concerned with individualizing educational programs for the gifted and will aid in achieving the goal of appropriate specialized instruction for gifted students.

A compilation of commercial educational materials suitable for gifted students has long been needed. Therefore, this text is written for educators and all others concerned with providing appropriate education for the gifted. It is written because of gifted students.

1 The Nature and Needs of the Gifted

The rationale for this book stems from our belief that gifted students are exceptional individuals who need and must have learning experiences beyond those typically offered in the general education program. Only then can they realize fully their potential for personal fulfillment, and only then can society benefit. These gifted individuals possess such exceptionally superior abilities that they can perform and achieve in one or more areas of endeavor. Such multiple gifts and talents are found in every culture and socioeconomic stratum in a variety of forms that include superior intelligence, academic talent, creativity, exceptional ability in the fine or performing arts, and outstanding social and leadership ability.

If talents and gifts such as these are to be developed and enhanced, specialized educational provisions and learning experiences must be given to these students, according to their individual needs. Otherwise, there is the risk that development may never occur. This would be a tremendous personal loss to the individual and a loss to society. Our society, with its increasingly critical social, scientific, technical, political, and personal problems, cannot afford such a loss of ability and talent which are so urgently needed. The goal of providing appropriate learning experiences for gifted students is consistent with our traditional national commitment to individual rights and equal opportunities for all. All students, including those who are gifted, should have the right to an education that is specifically designed to aid them in the development of their maximum potential.

One way of providing appropriate learning experiences for gifted students is to utilize appropriate educational methods and instructional materials with them. Educational methods and materials need to be geared to their ability and interest level rather than grade level. The instructional materials, resources, and teaching suggestions set forth in this book are specifically intended for elementary and secondary school students who have the potential for outstanding intellectual, creative, and academic performance.

WHO ARE GIFTED STUDENTS?

Gifted students possess such superior intellectual abilities and potential for outstanding achievement in comparison with the total student population that they need differentiated educational experiences if they are to realize this unique potential.

In addition to superior intellectual and academic ability, gifted stu-

3

dents may also be talented and/or creative. Talented students have truly exceptional abilities in specific areas of the fine and performing arts. Creative students possess the unique ability consistently to produce and elaborate upon original ideas and modes of expression. Such creative individuals eventually may evidence their talents in such diverse fields as the fine and performing arts; literary expression; scientific, technological, and mathematical pursuits; business, managerial, and political endeavors; and in social, educational, and humanitarian services. Such students may display any one of a variety of characteristics which would allow an alert parent, teacher, counselor, administrator, or other student to identify them as gifted. Frequently, parents think their child might be gifted because of signs of precocious development in preschool years. Gifted children often begin reading at an early age, sometimes as early as three or four, and frequently appear to teach themselves. Early development in other areas, such as speech and walking, may be advanced. In many cases their desire to learn can be seen early in childhood by their constant stream of questions, enjoyment of learning, and retention of knowledge.

Many gifted students display an almost insatiable curiosity. They appear to learn most things quickly and easily, without the need for drill and repetition. Their powers of reasoning, making comparisons and generalizations, and seeing relationships are usually strong. They tend to grasp concepts and processes more rapidly than others.

Typically, these students show a strong desire to learn, as well as persistence, if learning experiences are commensurate with their interests and level of ability. Gifted students often display keen powers of perception and observation. This means that they can frequently detect fallacies and inconsistencies. Original ideas and approaches to solving problems may be displayed. Independence in thought and action may also be seen. Frequently, verbal expression, vocabulary, and communicative abilities are quite strong.

Other characteristics that may be seen in gifted students are a sense of humor, a search for truth, a sense of justness and fairness, qualities of leadership, tendencies to classify and impose order, the building of collections, and a tolerance for uncertainty. Younger gifted students may have reading achievement test scores that are several years above grade level, while math and spelling achievement test scores may be somewhat lower than the reading scores. This is particularly true if math instruction is limited to grade-level activities and if the students read a great deal on their own. Reading comprehension is usually at a high level.

Powers of concentration while pursuing a subject of interest are typically strong, as well as retention of facts and ideas. Such students may display enjoyment of intellectual activities and an appreciation for many things of which other children may be unaware. The nature and frequency of questions posed by gifted students may reveal a high degree of insight and desire to understand.

Certainly, not all of these characteristics are displayed by all gifted students. However, observation of a number of these traits in an individual can provide clues to possible giftedness.

When attempting to detect characteristics that may indicate that a particular student is gifted, one should remember that gifted students can come from disadvantaged as well as advantaged backgrounds. Otherwise one may fail to observe many behaviors that provide evidence of possible giftedness. It is certainly not always true, but it is highly possible, that gifted and talented students from culturally diverse backgrounds and lower socioeconomic families have not had the same opportunities to develop and express their intelligence and talents that more advantaged children have had from a very early age.

These children may have parents who place little emphasis upon intellectual development and the enhancement of particular abilities and talents. Perhaps, because of economic pressures, their parents have simply not had the time to spend with their children that more financially secure parents have had. Frequently, these children have not been exposed to as many books and educational experiences as have more advantaged children. Therefore, they typically do not perform as well on conventional measures of intelligence because they have not had the types of experiences that enhance the abilities tapped by such tests. Children who come from culturally different backgrounds may have gifts and talents that are valued in their own society, but not ones on which the dominant society places a high premium.

Whatever the reasons, gifted students from different cultural backgrounds and lower socioeconomic families frequently do not display typical signs of giftedness observed in gifted students from more advantaged backgrounds. Teachers, counselors, administrators, program directors, and all those who are truly concerned with the development and enhancement of exceptional talents and gifts in the educational system, must be cognizant of the fact that gifted students can come from diverse backgrounds and all strata of society. In attempting to locate gifted students in the schools, special consideration must be given to the identification of gifted students from diverse backgrounds.

Handicapped students, including those with physical, visual, and hearing impairments, as well as those with emotional/behavioral problems and those with specific learning disabilities, may also be gifted. It is important that handicapping conditions do not inhibit the identification of a student as gifted.

Gifted females, especially those in the adolescent and junior and senior high years, may attempt to hide their intelligence and abilities because of social pressures or their fear of losing popularity or femininity. Hopefully, the changing roles and expectations for women will impede the concealment of their gifts and talents. Teachers, counselors, parents, and other concerned individuals should encourage the development of exceptional abilities and talents in gifted female students and aid them in accepting the fact that giftedness is not unfeminine nor a hindrance to social acceptance.

Some behaviors and traits of gifted students may be unacceptable to teachers, administrators, other educational personnel, and parents. Gifted students are more likely to display behaviors displeasing to teachers if the educational setting emphasizes drill and repetitious activities geared to grade-level expectations. The lack of challenge and subsequent boredom may produce disruptive behavior, inattention, disinterest, demands of relevancy, questions, arguments, or challenge to authority. Other gifted students may withdraw into their own personal world, initiate their own activities, and isolate themselves from an educational environment that has little to offer them.

It is not unusual for educators to feel threatened by gifted students and perhaps, subconsciously, to resent them. These typically sensitive students are quick to perceive this and may react with hostility or introversion, or possible conformity to expectations. Peer and parental pressures may trigger similar reactions.

Other traits that may be viewed as negative are stubbornness, an intolerance for erroneous or subjective statements and ideas, and questioning of traditional beliefs, ideas, and values. They may be critical and outspoken. They may be extremely persistent in the pursuit of a personal project.

Negative behaviors, however, are generally the exception. The majority of gifted students are well-adjusted, popular, cooperative, and a joy to teach.

Gifted students also may experience personal problems. They face the same kinds of problems faced by other students, in addition to problems at least partially caused by their exceptional abilities and talents. This is particularly true if their abilities are vastly superior to those of others with whom they are associated.

Gifted students may be subjected to unusual pressures to achieve and perform successfully. These pressures may come from parents, educators, and even from themselves. Gifted students, who have often succeeded easily in so many things, may set unrealistically high goals for themselves, and subsequently experience frustration when these goals are not quickly and easily attained. They may degrade themselves. They may avoid situations that pose any threat of possible failure.

Just as they question ideas, they question themselves. These students may perceive that they are different from other students. Instead of viewing these differences as positive, gifted students may perceive them as negative, particularly in a society that values conformity.

Finally, since many myths persist concerning gifted students, something should be said about these stereotypes which, in many cases, are not true. Gifted students are not necessarily straight *A* students or even high achievers. It is also true that straight *A* students and high achievers are not necessarily gifted. Because educational experiences often are not commensurate with their abilities, gifted students are frequently underachievers. Underachievement may result not only from lack of challenge and boredom, but also from handicapping conditions such as specific learning disabilities or emotional problems. While many gifted students are underachievers based on social expectations of their abilities, others with learning disabilities or emotional problems may be underachievers in comparison with their chronological age group. It is important to realize that these students may also be gifted and to develop educational programs that meet their unique needs.

Gifted students are not social outcasts in the majority of cases. Typically, they are popular and are often leaders. Most gifted students are not intellectual snobs and bookworms. They are often well-rounded and possess a variety of interests. Gifted students certainly do not all come from wealthy families, yet this idea still persists.

Perhaps the most detrimental myth of all is that gifted students will achieve on their own initiative. They may very well achieve on their own, but it is unlikely that they will reach their maximum potential without specialized, individualized educational provisions designed and implemented to enhance their truly exceptional abilities and talents.

INSTRUCTIONAL NEEDS OF GIFTED STUDENTS

The most imperative educational need of gifted students is that they be given learning experiences that are consistent with their capabilities and developmental level. For gifted students, grade-level assignments may not only impede their achievement, but may also produce negative connotations of formal education. Drill and repetition of activities already understood can only produce boredom, dislike of school, and underdeveloped potential abilities.

Gifted students are frequently capable of assuming at least some responsibility for their own education. They often can analyze their own needs, interests, and abilities. Therefore, many learning tasks may be student-initiated rather than teacher-initiated.

Students who are gifted need to learn processes and concepts that are applicable to a variety of situations rather than simply to memorize numerous facts. They may need aid in developing logical thinking skills and reasoning. Library research techniques should be introduced early in the educational process so that gifted students may learn and investigate on their own. The scientific method of research can also be taught to young gifted students. Critical thinking skills, creative problem solving, and effective means of communication are also important educational concerns for gifted students. Analysis, synthesis, and evaluation of ideas and thoughts should be emphasized as means for the development of higher cognitive processes.

It is also true that we cannot stereotype the instructional needs of gifted students. The gifted are a heterogeneous group with various abilities, needs, interests, and characteristics. Their instructional needs are also quite diverse.

Individual gifted students have their own particular learning styles or ways in which they learn most effectively. Some have an auditory learning style. They learn best when information is presented verbally through conversations, lectures, tapes, records, et cetera. Others have a visual learning style and learn best when they can see the process or information, such as through concrete visual aids, pictures, and observation. Some of these students prefer to learn independently, while others prefer group learning experiences. Individual learning styles should be taken into consideration in program planning and materials selection for gifted students.

The interests of the gifted vary greatly and should also be taken into account in designing appropriate learning experiences for them. This can usually be achieved when gifted students are allowed to decide and assume responsibility for some of their educational experiences.

The abilities of gifted students also differ among individuals. Not only will differences exist in the overall level of ability, but also in patterns of abilities and relative strengths and weaknesses. These abilities should be determinants in the choice of appropriate learning experiences and instructional materials for gifted students.

Special Programs for Gifted Students   An increasing number of schools are establishing special programs for gifted students in order to provide more appropriate learning experiences for them and to allow them to develop their potential. Several program alternatives exist, and selection of any one or a combination of them should depend on the students to be served and the material and human resources available.

Early school admission may be a viable alternative where state legislation permits. *Acceleration* and *grade skipping* have proved to be successful in many cases. For acceleration, grade skipping, and early school admission to be successful, the individual student's abilities, needs, and intellectual, social, and emotional characteristics must be carefully considered. Acceleration has been quite beneficial for many gifted students, especially those who are highly gifted. In the majority of cases, acceleration has not been detrimental to social and emotional development. Yet, the decision to accelerate an individual student should not be made without careful consideration by educators, parents, and the student.

The provision of *advanced study* or course-work can be possible, even in elementary schools where the necessary resources are available. Courses in foreign languages and advanced studies in science, math, social studies, creative writing, debate, and other fields may be offered. Many colleges and universities and some foundations both here and abroad now offer special *summer programs* and/or *Saturday programs* for gifted students, providing them with opportunities for specialized or advanced study. Some programs may be limited to certain age or grade ranges, but most are offered for both elementary and secondary students. In some locales *before-school or after-school special programs* are provided.

There are also several options for advanced study which are particularly pertinent at the secondary level. *Advanced placement* courses offer a student the opportunity to study a subject on the college level while still enrolled in high school, and if a student achieves a sufficient score on a final examination, he or she may earn college credit. *Early admission to college,* when possible, may be the alternative of choice for some gifted students. As with early admission to school, careful consideration is advised when making such a decision. Social and emotional factors, as well as intellectual ones, should be weighed in the decision-making process. Early admission to college has been successful for many gifted students, particularly for those who are highly gifted. *Dual enrollment* in college and in high school may be possible for gifted students who live in areas close to the college or university.

Independent study allows gifted students to pursue projects in depth and to learn research, writing, investigation, and communication techniques. Teachers may serve as resource guides in selecting appropriate topics for study, sources of information, research methods, and clear writing and communication techniques, and in aiding students in locating appropriate outlets for their products. An organized, ongoing program of independent study, rather than isolated opportunities, should be established if this is to be considered a programming alternative for gifted students.

The *mentor approach* can be a successful means of providing appropriate learning experience for gifted students. A mentor is someone with expertise in a field of interest to an individual student. The mentor then agrees to aid the student in the study and exploration of the chosen subject. In most cases, the mentor is someone within the community or surrounding area who meets regularly with the student. Mentors can provide needed learning experiences to students who are exceptionally talented in visual or performing arts, as well as to gifted students with particular interests in a chosen academic field of study. Similar to the mentor approach is an *internship* program where a student spends a specified period of time working and studying with a professional or expert in a chosen field. During this time the student is usually on sabbatical from regular classes.

Special resource room programs are being established for gifted students in many school systems. With these types of programs, students typically spend the majority of school time in the regular classroom and a specified amount of time each week in the resource program with other gifted students and a teacher with knowledge and/or training in teaching the gifted.

Special classes or full-time school programs may be formed for gifted students. Full-time special classes can be designed especially for students who are highly gifted and in such cases where the educational needs of these students are so different from those of the general school population that they learn more effectively in a special class.

Full time *special schools* for gifted or talented students have been established in some states and cities. These schools are frequently designed for secondary students, and courses of study are usually concentrated in specialized areas, such as the fine and performing arts and science and technology.

In all cases the type of programs instituted for gifted students should be based on careful consideration of feasible alternatives, the human, material, and financial resources available, and, most important, the educational needs of the students to be served. Programs should be designed to fit student needs. Students should not be made to fit into particular programs. In some cases, the diversity of the needs, interests, and abilities of gifted students in a particular school or school system may require that several program alternatives be established in order to provide optimal learning experiences for all gifted students.

When designing and implementing instructional programs for gifted students, state guidelines and policies should be taken into account. These vary from state to state, but often program options, identification guidelines, teacher certification requirements, and funding levels are established by the state. Some states require that individual education plans or other educational accountability plans be written for gifted students.

INSTRUCTIONAL ADAPTATIONS FOR GIFTED STUDENTS IN THE REGULAR CLASSROOM

Although the number of specialized programs being established for gifted students is increasing, the majority of these students remain in regular classrooms. Typically, students in resource programs for the gifted still spend most of their school time in the regular classroom. Therefore, it is important that instructional adaptations be made in the regular education program in order to provide for the unique instructional needs of the gifted. A variety of educational adaptations can be made, but the choice should depend upon the unique needs, abilities, and interests of the individual student. Other considerations might be the instructional style and particular capabilities and areas of expertise of the teacher; other resource persons; available material; library and audiovisual resources; community resources; and the abilities, needs, and interests of other gifted children in the classroom. Many instructional adaptations for gifted students in the regular school program can be made at little or no expense.

Gifted students may be allowed to pursue *independent study* in an area of interest. Topics for study may be selected by the student and approved by the teacher or may be jointly selected by student and teacher. The teacher may then serve as a resource person and guide, suggesting research methods, sources of information, and means of communicating findings. The teacher may suggest means by which the results of independent study may be disseminated or displayed.

If there are several gifted students in the classroom, the teacher may encourage them to undertake *small group projects* in areas of mutual interest. For small group projects, the teacher may serve as a resource person and guide as with independent study projects.

The *mentor approach* may also be used by regular classroom teachers who instruct gifted students. The teacher can solicit the assistance of a person with expertise in an area of interest to a gifted student so that the student can pursue learning experiences under the mentor's guidance. If no such person is locally available, the teacher may help the gifted student to locate someone knowledgeable in the field with whom they can correspond. *Internship* programs may also be considered.

The *contract method* can be used effectively to provide appropriate learning experiences for gifted students. The teacher and the individual student jointly decide on a topic of study and the requirements that should be met to complete the project successfully. They also mutually agree on deadlines, the amount of classroom time which may be utilized, the means of presenting the results of the project, and the method of evaluating the project. Both the student and the teacher sign the contract as a mutual agreement. Contracts allow gifted students to assume responsibility for their own learning experiences.

Creative teachers can implement these suggested adaptations in a variety of ways in order to provide learning experiences for gifted students which are specific to their interest and ability levels rather than grade levels. Any adaptations for gifted students should emphasize the development of higher cognitive and affective skills; thinking, reasoning, decision-making, and problem-solving capabilities; and the learning of processes and generalizations. Instructional provisions for gifted students must allow for their active participation in the learning process to insure that they become originators as well as consumers of knowledge.

2 Materials Selection for Gifted Students

While it is the purpose of this book to provide a compilation of suggested commercial educational materials for gifted students, we do not advocate that educational programs for gifted students be based solely on the use of commercially prepared materials. However, when commercial materials are used, deciding which materials would be most appropriate should be based on careful consideration of a number of basic factors. Specifically, students' interests, educational needs, prior experiences, learning styles, developmental levels, and abilities should be of primary concern. The educational goals of the program should be considered, as well as monies available, and the cost-effectiveness of the materials. Materials selection should be based on the unique learning needs of gifted students, as well as on individual student needs. The instructional style and particular capabilities of the teacher are additional factors to be considered. While commercially prepared materials should not be utilized to meet every student and program need, they can be a valuable asset to program development when careful thought is given to the selection process.

CRITERIA FOR THE SELECTION OF EDUCATIONAL MATERIALS FOR GIFTED STUDENTS

In order to facilitate the analysis of instructional materials under consideration for use in educational programs for gifted students, a checklist entitled "Criteria for the Selection of Educational Materials for Gifted Students" has been designed (see Table 1). This checklist has three basic components: General Considerations in Materials Selection, Student Considerations in Materials Selection, and Teacher Considerations in Materials Selection. General Considerations are applicable for the selection of all educational materials. Student Considerations pertain specifically to the educational needs of gifted students. This portion of the checklist is designed to be the most helpful in determining whether a material promotes or allows for differentiated educational experiences for gifted students. Teacher Considerations are designed to promote the selection of those materials that will enhance the role of the instructor as a facilitator of the learning process. This checklist is not viewed as all-inclusive. Additional items may be added to the checklist to meet local considerations.

This checklist is designed not as an evaluation instrument but rather as a screening device. The number of positive and negative responses should not determine final selection or rejection of a particular material, as no material will contain all facets incorporated into the checklist. The selection of a specific educational material should be based on positive responses to those items that best express student, program, and teacher needs.

SUGGESTIONS FOR LOCAL USE OF THE MATERIALS CHECKLIST

Modification of the checklist for the selection of educational materials for gifted students to meet local or individual program needs is encouraged. This checklist should not be perceived as all-inclusive. It is intended to serve as a guide to materials selection, and the questions included are suggested ones for consideration.

In some cases items that reflect particular program goals may be added. In other cases, educators at the local level may wish to delete certain items and retain those they perceive to be the most important.

Numerical ratings have been intentionally omitted from this checklist. We feel that including a rating scale would usurp professional judgment at the local level. Teachers and administrators of programs for gifted students may wish to devise their own rating system to use with this checklist. When this is done at the local level, materials can then be rated and subsequently selected to fit individual program goals and objectives.

TABLE 1   CRITERIA FOR THE SELECTION OF EDUCATIONAL MATERIALS FOR GIFTED STUDENTS

General Considerations in Materials Selection	Yes	No
Does the material include general learning objectives?	——	——
Do the learning objectives of the material support the goals of the program?	——	——
Are the concepts presented in the materials valid?	——	——

Does the material have an attractive format and design? ___ ___

Are the materials durable? ___ ___

Are the materials conveniently packaged? ___ ___

Are the materials portable? ___ ___

Are the majority of the materials nonconsumable? ___ ___

Is the cost of the material commensurate with the use and learning objectives? ___ ___

Is the necessary equipment available for the utilization of the material? ___ ___

Is the purchase of additional materials necessary? ___ ___

Is the suggested grade or age level specified? ___ ___

Is the material designed to be used individually? ___ ___

Is the material appropriate for group instruction? ___ ___

Is an instructional guide provided? ___ ___

Are there sufficient numbers of students to utilize the material? ___ ___

Are the learning materials presented in sequence? ___ ___

Has the material been field tested? ___ ___

Do the learning objectives justify the amount of time required for the activity? ___ ___

Do the concepts presented in the materials conflict with community standards? ___ ___

Are the materials presented in such a way so as to be nondiscriminatory in terms of culture, race, sex, or handicapping condition? ___ ___

Student Considerations in Materials Selection for Gifted Students

	Yes	No

Are the students' interests reflected in the material? ___ ___

Is the mode of presentation commensurate with the learning style of the student? ___ ___

Can the concepts presented be employed by the student in other learning situations? ___ ___

Is self-evaluation an integral part of the material? ___ ___

Do the materials encourage the student to undertake further study and research in related areas? ___ ___

Are appropriate references provided for use by the student? ___ ___

Student Considerations in Materials Selection for Gifted Students (continued)	Yes	No

Are the processes taught applicable to a variety of learning situations? ⎯⎯ ⎯⎯

Is the content of the material consistent with the student's developmental level or prior experience or training in this area rather than grade-level oriented? ⎯⎯ ⎯⎯

Do students develop products, and if so, are appropriate outlets for students' products suggested? ⎯⎯ ⎯⎯

Does the material promote development in one or more dimensions of learning appropriate for the gifted? ⎯⎯ ⎯⎯

   A. Does the material foster and enhance the development of oral and written communication skills? ⎯⎯ ⎯⎯

   B. Does the material foster and enhance the development of higher cognitive processes of analysis, synthesis, and evaluation? ⎯⎯ ⎯⎯

   C. Does the material foster and enhance the development in the affective domain such as understanding ourselves and others? ⎯⎯ ⎯⎯

   D. Does the material foster and enhance the development of logical thinking, such as inductive and deductive reasoning, and problem-solving skills? ⎯⎯ ⎯⎯

   E. Does the material foster and enhance the development of critical thinking, such as the judgment and decision-making processes? ⎯⎯ ⎯⎯

   F. Does the material foster and enhance the development of divergent production, such as open-ended responses and self-expression? ⎯⎯ ⎯⎯

   G. Does the material foster and enhance research skills, such as library research skills, and knowledge and application of the scientific method of research? ⎯⎯ ⎯⎯

   H. Does the material foster and enhance development in values clarification such as defining, expressing, and assuming responsibility for personal values? ⎯⎯ ⎯⎯

Student Considerations in Materials Selection for Gifted Students (continued)	Yes	No
I. Does the material foster and enhance the development of group dynamics, group interaction processes, and communication and discussion techniques?	——	——
J. Does the material foster and enhance the development of creativity, such as fluency, flexibility, originality, and elaboration?	——	——

Teacher Considerations in Materials Selection for Gifted Students	Yes	No
Are specific teaching suggestions provided?	——	——
Do materials allow for teacher initiative and adaption?	——	——
Are guidelines given for making some of the necessary materials rather than purchasing them?	——	——
If specialized training is required for teacher utilization of materials, do instructions accompany the material?	——	——
Is the amount of required teacher preparation time consistent with the scope of the learning objectives?	——	——
Are appropriate references and resources suggested?	——	——
Is the teaching style suggested in the materials parallel with the instructional style of the teacher?	——	——
Are suggestions provided for the evaluation of student progress?	——	——

CAUTIONS IN MATERIALS SELECTION
FOR GIFTED STUDENTS

Certain cautions are advised in the selection of commercial educational materials for gifted students. Materials marked "enrichment" should be carefully examined to determine the nature of the educational objective. Enrichment activities appropriate to the gifted should extend learning experiences and not reinforce concepts already mastered. Some enrichment materials which are attractively packaged lack depth and challenge.

Materials with specific indicators of age and/or grade level should be analyzed to determine if their content is appropriate to the development level, abilities, and interests of a gifted student. Using materials designed for particular grade levels at lower grade levels does not, in itself, constitute an appropriate educational program for gifted students. The overuse of games and puzzles in programming for the gifted is discouraged, as well as the sole use of commercial instructional materials. Educational materials should not constitute the total instructional program for gifted students. The manner in which materials are utilized, adapted, and supplemented by teachers determines the direction, focus, and quality of differentiated programs for the gifted. These students should be allowed to assume responsibility for their own learning, including content, learning style, and rate.

3 Selected Instructional Materials for Gifted Elementary and Secondary School Students

Commercial educational materials recommended or selected as appropriate for gifted students in the elementary and secondary school grades are compiled in Table 2, along with objective descriptions of each material. Materials are listed in the major content areas of language arts, math, science, and social studies. A few materials spanning several content areas are listed as multidisciplinary. In addition, materials are listed in several other areas of study designated as appropriate for the gifted. These include: creativity; debate; futurism; group dynamics; leadership, logic, critical thinking, and problem solving; research; and values clarification. Although only a few materials are listed under the category of leadership, many materials listed under the categories of group dynamics, debate, and values clarification are often effective in promoting leadership abilities.

Basal materials and textbook series found in the general curriculum are not included, since the major purpose of this handbook is to list materials that can expand present curricular offerings. There are so many books and other reading matter that provide enjoyment and learning experience for gifted students that it would be an impossible task to try to list them. Films and equipment are also excluded. Educational materials produced locally, not available commercially, are not included—it would be impossible to include them all.

The majority of materials compiled in Table 2 were not specifically designed for the gifted. A large percentage have been used with the gifted, however, and reports indicate that they have been successful. Creative teachers may wish to adapt them to individual students' needs.

ADAPTATION OF COMMERCIAL MATERIALS FOR GIFTED STUDENTS

There are relatively few commercial materials designed for gifted students; therefore, adaptations of available materials may be necessary and should be based on a careful examination of the instructional materials, taking into consideration the needs, interests, and abilities of the gifted students being taught.

In adapting these materials, content must be restructured to incorporate concepts, thinking skills, cognitive processes, and other dimensions of learning that are appropriate for gifted students. Materials listed in Table 2 incorporate several dimensions of learning necessary to differentiate instruction for gifted students. These included dimensions are marked in the table. Materials lacking specific dimensions of learning can be restructured to include those necessary for individual student development.

Materials might be adapted to enhance students' *oral communications skills* by having students design and portray individual or group presentations, incorporating such areas as multimedia demonstration, debates, role playing, simulations, competitions, speeches, and plays. Written communication skills may be extended through compositions, creative writing activities, including poetry, plays, short stories, and other literary works.

The assignments and learning activities may be designed or restructured to promote the development of the *higher cognitive processes* of analysis, synthesis, and evaluation. Students may analyze information in textbooks, instructional materials, and other educational resources, synthesize this with previously acquired knowledge or disciplines, and formulate judgments and opinions.

Values clarification strategies appropriate for the gifted should focus on knowledge of one's own values and acceptance of responsibility for individual values. Activities designed to foster this may be incorporated into educational activities through the utilization of the cognitive content of materials. Students should be encouraged to explore and express their values pertinent to scientific and technological advances, historical and contemporary events, literary and artistic works, as well as in other areas of the curriculum.

Affective development activities may build upon and extend values clarification by assisting the student to understand, relate, and respond to others' value systems, which may be different from their own. Through group discussions and explorations of different values, students' development in the affective domain will be elevated.

Logical thinking skills may be developed through the incorporation of questions and assignments that require utilization of orderly thinking processes and problem-solving techniques. Activities to foster the development of deductive reasoning abilities might be assigned so that students could deduce the correct answer, given information or facts. Inductive reasoning skills can be developed by guiding students to understand underlying rules and principles which apply to various situations.

Critical thinking skills may be effectuated by allowing students to analyze critically and evaluate topics of study. Students should be encouraged to base judgments on factual information and logical thinking processes.

To foster the skill of *divergent production,* students should be encouraged to explore alternatives and possible solutions. Divergent production may be included in written and oral expression, as well as other areas. This skill may be incorporated into individual activities, as well as in group brainstorming sessions.

Research skills, both scientific and library research techniques, can be improved through the incorporation of individual and group research into selected topics of interest. This also allows for in-depth student exploration of particular interest areas.

The fostering of *group dynamics* may be undertaken through the freedom of group discussions. Students may need guidance in the formulation and implementation of guidelines that foster effective interchange of ideas and consensus.

The element of *creativity* and its expression may be added to materials and assignments by promoting the formulation and expression of all possible alternatives, expanding ideas, altering mind-sets, and posing original ideas and solutions. The principles of fluency, flexibility, originality, and elaboration may be incorporated into all content areas, as well as the areas of fine and performing arts.

Commercial materials may be adapted to make them more appropriate for use with gifted students by using only parts of the materials and by eliminating repetitious components and activities, to provide a vertical, rather than a lateral, learning progression. This may be accomplished by designing pretest assessment instruments to determine the appropriate entry level into the material. Teachers may find that materials designed for older students are suitable for younger gifted students if the appropriate dimensions of learning have been incorporated into the materials. Also important in adapting materials is the learning style of the student. Materials may be restructured to parallel the style of the individual gifted student, thus assuring maximum learning experiences.

Educational materials may be supplemented through the incorporation of additional material resources, including books and audiovisuals. Free and inexpensive materials, which may be added to presently available commercially prepared materials, are usually available from businesses, industries, government agencies, and other community resources. Persons with expertise in particular areas may be consulted to expand the knowledge base of the material. Several materials and resources complementing the materials may be combined in a learning center, either in a regular classroom or in a specialized program for the gifted.

Educational activities and projects may be altered for gifted students by presenting questions pertinent to possible future situations, by incorporating values clarification and affective development strat egies, by utilization of creative problem-solving techniques, and by exploration of careers and possible future careers which are commensurate with the abilities and interests of the individual gifted students. Instructional projects for gifted students should, whenever possible, seek to effectuate thinking skills and incorporate higher cognitive processes.

Individual and group research projects allow gifted students to explore in depth areas of particular interest. Students may undertake library research and scientific research and experimentation. Field visits, correspondence, and personal interviews constitute additional sources of information for students doing research.

Materials may be extended by having students design and present individual and/or group presentations on particular topics of interest. Such presentations may include such areas as multimedia demonstrations, debates, role playing, competitions, plays, research projects, and scientific experiments. In addition, application of content may be formulated into original games and simulations, or existing games may be adapted with rule changes and alternate strategies.

Incorporating the suggestions for materials adaptations will aid both the regular classroom teacher and the specialized teacher of gifted students in providing differentiated education appropriate to the needs, abilities, interests, and learning styles of the gifted learner. In addition, gifted students may have their own suggestions for adapting materials.

GUIDE TO THE USE OF THE ANALYSIS CHART

In order to facilitate the objective examination and selection of materials for gifted students, an analysis chart was constructed. The intent of the chart is to give a description of the purpose of the materials, the format, and the component parts. It is not intended to serve as a subjective evaluation.

The analysis chart is divided into six major components: publisher/distributor, approximate cost, approximate age level, dimensions of learning, format, and the major components of the materials. The name of the publisher of the material is listed on the chart. In a few cases, distributors are listed. Complete addresses of these publishers and distributors are provided at the end of this chapter. The approximate cost of the material was obtained from the publisher or distributor, but purchasing prices may vary according to location and the availability of the material. The age ranges provided are merely suggested ones for gifted students and may not coincide with the manufacturer's or distributor's suggested age or grade levels. Age ranges also may vary widely according to the abilities and interests of individual gifted students. Approximate age ranges are listed according to the following code:

P—Primary   (Grades 1-4)
I—Intermediate   (Grades 5-8)
S—Secondary   (Grades 9-12)

Dimensions of Learning

This section of Table 2 serves as a guide to the specific areas of learning appropriate to the gifted. Following is an explanation of each.

Communication Skills materials focus on a variety of means for the oral and written expression of ideas, concepts, and knowledge. The activities contained in these materials are designed to enhance students' abilities to communicate their ideas to others.

Cognitive Development materials stress the higher cognitive processes of analysis, synthesis, and evaluation of ideas, processes, and products with minimal emphasis on rote learning. These materials focus on the development and enhancement of thinking skills. These skills, once mastered, can be applied to any area of study.

Affective Development materials foster knowledge of self; social awareness; and responding and relating to others, their needs, and value systems. The objectives of these materials are to foster higher levels of development in the affective domain. Understanding of self and understanding and relating to others are the primary goals.

Logical Thinking materials contribute to the development of orderly and sequential thought processes, deductive and inductive reasoning, and their application to problem solving. Emphasis is given to the development of thinking processes rather than on the acquisition of factual knowledge. Logical thinking skills can be applied to any area of study or problem-solving situations.

Critical Thinking materials enhance the ability of the students to evaluate and to critically analyze ideas and information. Judgment, based upon factual material and logical thought processes, is fostered.

Divergent Production materials encourage the formulation and expression of many possible solutions, thoughts, and ideas. Students are encouraged to use their imaginations and creative thought processes in the generation of new ideas or solutions to problems.

Research Skills materials aid students in conducting their own research or in developing research skills. Research is broadly defined to include both library and scientific research techniques. These materials allow students to acquire the skills necessary to assume responsibility for their own learning. The techniques of gathering and evaluating information are emphasized.

Values Clarification materials assist the individual in defining, expressing, and assuming responsibility for personal values. Students are encouraged to develop and define their own values rather than merely conforming to the values of others without careful thought. Individual responsibility for one's own values is emphasized.

Group Dynamics materials seek to develop group interaction processes, verbal and nonverbal communication, discussion techniques, and consensus formulation. Students are urged to express their ideas and to listen to the ideas of others. Group evaluation of ideas and consensus in decision-making is stressed.

Creativity materials strive to develop fluency, flexibility, originality, and elaboration in thinking, writing, speaking, artistic expression, products development, and problem solving. The objectives of these materials are to foster and enhance the formulation and expression of a variety of unique ideas and to build upon these ideas.

For each instructional material listed in Table 2, those dimensions of learning that reflect the objectives of the material are marked, based on the stated instructional objectives and evaluation of the educational activities of the material. In many cases, creative teachers can modify a material to include other dimensions of learning. Marking, however, was based on utilization of the material without modification.

The number of dimensions of learning marked do not necessarily reflect the quality of a material. Some excellent materials are designed with more narrowly focused sets of objectives, yet educational activities are well constructed and developed to meet these objectives.

Teachers and program administrators at the local level should compare the goals and objectives of their programs for gifted students with the dimensions of learning. They can then look more closely at those materials that emphasize the specific dimensions of learning that are most congruent with the objectives of individual programs and the needs of the students they serve.

Teachers and administrators may find that many of the books of brainteasers, puzzles, and games listed in Chapter 5 can be appropriately included in educational programs for gifted students. Since these books, puzzles, and games are described in a separate chapter, they are not listed here.

Materials Format Materials in Table 2 are marked for individual instruction and/or group instruction. Most materials designated as appropriate for group instruction are intended for small group learning situations. It should be noted, however, that some of the simulations cited require larger groups. A few materials may be used for either individual or group instruction.

Components of Materials Material components have been divided into the following parts: kit, workbook, worksheets, taskcards, filmstrips, slides, audio tapes, books, records, instructional game, specialized equipment, instructional guide, simulation, transparencies, duplicating masters, and other visual aids. Other visual aids may consist of posters, charts, graphs, or pictures.

TABLE 2   COMMERCIAL MATERIALS LISTING

Company and Materials	Cost (Approx.)	Level (Sugg.)	Communication Skills	Cognitive Development	Affective Development	Logical Thinking	Critical Thinking	Divergent Production	Research Skills	Values Clarification	Group Dynamics	Creativity	Individual Instruction	Group Instruction	Kit	Workbook	Worksheets	Taskcards	Filmstrip(s)	Slides	Audio Tape(s)	Book(s)	Record(s)	Instructional Game	Specialized Equipment	Instructional Guide	Simulation	Other Visual Aids	Duplicating Masters	Transparencies
LANGUAGE ARTS																														
Ann Arbor Publishers, Inc.																														
Critical Reading Primers: Books A, B, C, and D	$17.00	P	x	x									x			x										x				
Creative Publications																														
Think! Draw! Write!	12.00	P	x	x		x	x					x	x													x				x
Creative Teaching Press, Inc.																														
Desk Top Story Starters	5.00	P	x				x						x				x	x								x				x
Make Believe Story Starters	5.00	P	x				x						x				x	x								x				x
Super Size Story Starters	5.00	P	x				x						x				x	x								x				x

TABLE 2 COMMERCIAL MATERIALS LISTING (continued)

Company and Materials	Cost (Approx.)	Level (Sugg.)	Dimensions of Learning										Format		Components															
			Communication Skills	Cognitive Development	Affective Development	Logical Thinking	Critical Thinking	Divergent Production	Research Skills	Values Clarification	Group Dynamics	Creativity	Individual Instruction	Group Instruction	Kit	Workbook	Worksheets	Taskcards	Filmstrip(s)	Slides	Audio Tape(s)	Book(s)	Record(s)	Instructional Game	Specialized Equipment	Instructional Guide	Simulation	Other Visual Aids	Duplicating Masters	Transparencies
Curriculum Associates, Inc.																														
Story Starters—Primary	$ 12.00	P	x					x					x	x			x									x				
Working with Stories	11.00	P	x					x					x	x												x				x
Education Insights, Inc.																														
Story Sparkers	7.00	P	x	x	x			x					x	x			x									x				
Good Apple, Inc.																														
Creative Writing in Action	6.00	P	x					x					x	x	x											x				
Fact, Fantasy, and Folklore	10.00	P	x	x			x	x					x	x	x											x				
The Good Apple Creative Writing Book	8.00	P	x					x					x		x											x				
Institute for the Advancement of Philosophy for Children																														
Kio and Gus and Wondering at the World Manual	$ 37.00	P	x	x	x	x	x							x											x	x				
Milliken Publishing Co.																														
Creative Expression	10.00	P	x					x					x	x												x			x	x
Creative Language Projects	15.00	P	x					x					x	x												x			x	
Creative Writing	10.00	P	x					x					x	x												x			x	x
Penichet Publishing Co.																														
Reading to Discover Activity Cards	5.00	P	x	x			x	x					x	x				x								x				
Starting Your Stories Activity Cards	$ 5.00	P	x					x					x	x				x								x				
Prentice-Hall Media																														
First Experience in Creative Writing	75.00	P	x	x				x					x	x					x		x					x				
Frank Schaeffer Publications, Inc.																														
Creative Writing Activity Cards	6.00	P	x					x					x	x				x								x				
Troll Associates																														
Getting Ready to Write Creatively	120.00	P	x	x				x					x	x					x		x					x				
Let's Write—Descriptively	120.00	P	x	x				x					x	x					x		x				x					

TABLE 2   COMMERCIAL MATERIALS LISTING (continued)

Company and Materials	Cost (Approx.)	Level (Sugg.)	Dimensions of Learning										Format		Components															
			Communication Skills	Cognitive Development	Affective Development	Logical Thinking	Critical Thinking	Divergent Production	Research Skills	Values Clarification	Group Dynamics	Creativity	Individual Instruction	Group Instruction	Kit	Workbook	Worksheets	Taskcards	Filmstrip(s)	Slides	Audio Tape(s)	Book(s)	Record(s)	Instructional Game	Specialized Equipment	Instructional Guide	Simulation	Other Visual Aids	Duplicating Masters	Transparencies
Creative Publications																														
Think About It! Language Arts Problems of the Day	$ 9.00	P-I	x	x		x	x	x					x	x			x										x				
Curriculum Associates, Inc.																														
Story Starters—Intermediate	12.00	P-I	x			x							x	x				x									x				
Disseminators of Knowledge, Publishers																														
Effective Communication: A Handbook of Discussion Skills	3.00	P-I	x		x		x	x	x	x			x	x			x										x				
Educational Insights, Inc.																														
More Write On	7.00	P-I	x			x							x	x					x			x									
Goodyear Books																														
The Big Book of Independent Study	$19.00	P-I	x	x		x	x						x	x								x									
The Big Book of Writing	19.00	P-I	x	x		x							x	x								x									
Hayes School Publishing Co. Inc.																														
Language Arts Challengers for the Gifted	4.00	P-I	x	x		x	x						x	x													x		x		
Institute for the Advancement of Philosophy for Children																														
Pixie and Looking for Meaning Manual	37.00	P-I	x	x	x	x	x							x										x		x				
Charles E. Merrill Publishing Co.																														
The Productive Thinking Program	198.00	P-I	x	x		x	x	x					x	x	x	x						x	x			x			x	x
Milliken Publishing Co.																														
Creative Language Projects	15.00	P-I	x					x					x	x												x		x		
Creative Writing—Grades 4–6	$ 5.00	P-I	x					x					x	x												x		x	x	
Creative Writing—Grades 6–8	5.00	P-I	x					x					x	x												x		x	x	
WFF'N Proof Learning Games Associates																														
Propaganda Game	13.00	P-I	x	x		x	x				x		x	x										x	x	x				

TABLE 2   COMMERCIAL MATERIALS LISTING (continued)

Company and Materials	Cost (Approx.)	Level (Sugg.)	Dimensions of Learning										Format		Components															
			Communication Skills	Cognitive Development	Affective Development	Logical Thinking	Critical Thinking	Divergent Production	Research Skills	Values Clarification	Group Dynamics	Creativity	Individual Instruction	Group Instruction	Kit	Workbook	Worksheets	Taskcards	Filmstrip(s)	Slides	Audio Tape(s)	Book(s)	Record(s)	Instructional Game	Specialized Equipment	Instructional Guide	Simulation	Other Visual Aids	Duplicating Masters	Transparencies
Xerox Education Publications																														
Imagine and Write Program	$ 7.00	P-I	x				x						x	x	x															
Ann Arbor Publishers, Inc.																														
Critical Reading Series: Books A, B, C, and D	22.00	I	x	x									x			x										x				
The Center for the Humanities, Inc.																														
In Your Own Words: Learning to Write	220.00	I	x	x		x	x	x					x		x	x	x					x				x				
Special Problems in Library Research	220.00	I	x						x		x		x	x	x							x				x				
Using Library Resources and Reference Materials	220.00	I	x						x		x		x	x	x							x				x				
Charlotte's Web																														
Alphabetils	$ 15.00	I	x	x		x							x	x			x						x			x				
Coronet																														
Write in Style	90.00	I	x	x		x	x	x					x			x	x						x			x				x
Write Now!	105.00	I	x	x		x	x	x					x			x	x				x		x			x				x
Writing Sense	119.00	I	x	x		x	x	x					x			x	x				x		x			x				x
Writing Short Stories	89.00	I	x	x		x	x	x					x			x	x				x		x			x				
Creative Learning Systems, Inc.																														
Creative Cue Cards	30.00	I	x			x	x	x					x	x				x								x				
Educational Activities, Inc.																														
Cognitive Challenges in Language Arts	$ 39.00	I	x	x		x	x						x	x												x				x
Encyclopedia Brittanica Educational Corporation																														
Open Box: Ideas for Creative Expression	67.00	I	x					x					x	x	x							x	x			x	x			
Eye Gate Media																														
How to Write Reports	102.00	I	x	x					x				x	x							x		x			x				
Interact																														
Code	$ 11.00	I	x	x		x	x	x					x	x	x				x	x						x	x			

TABLE 2 COMMERCIAL MATERIALS LISTING (continued)

Company and Materials	Cost (Approx.)	Level (Sugg.)	Communication Skills	Cognitive Development	Affective Development	Logical Thinking	Critical Thinking	Divergent Production	Research Skills	Values Clarification	Group Dynamics	Creativity	Individual Instruction	Group Instruction	Kit	Workbook	Worksheets	Taskcards	Filmstrip(s)	Slides	Audio Tape(s)	Book(s)	Record(s)	Instructional Game	Specialized Equipment	Instructional Guide	Simulation	Other Visual Aids	Duplicating Masters	Transparencies
Locality	7.00	I	x	x	x	x	x	x	x				x			x	x									x				
Patterns: The How to Write A Poem Book	16.00	I	x	x	x	x	x	x		x		x	x										x			x				
Puzzle	18.00	I	x	x		x	x	x	x					x			x										x	x		
Sources	22.00	I	x	x	x	x	x		x				x		x											x				
Midwest Publications																														
Word Benders	13.00	I	x	x		x	x						x	x	x											x				
Penichet Publishing Co.																														
Imagination and Language (Creative Writing Experiences in the Imaginative Use of Language)	$ 8.00	I	x	x			x						x				x									x				
Xerox Education Publications																														
Mindgame: Experiences in Creative Writing	2.00	I	x	x			x						x			x	x										x			
The Center for the Humanities, Inc.																														
Creative Writing: Imagination and Self-Expression	220.00	I-S	x	x	x	x	x	x	x				x	x	x						x					x				
Speak Up: Skills of Oral Communication	$220.00	I-S	x	x		x	x	x					x	x	x						x					x				
Creative Learning Systems, Inc.																														
Cereals, Soaps and Sportcars	20.00	I-S	x				x	x					x		x	x	x									x				
Investigative Reporting	20.00	I-S	x				x	x							x	x	x									x				
Scriptwriter Lab Kit	55.00	I-S	x				x	x					x		x	x	x									x			x	
Spage Saga	20.00	I-S	x				x	x					x		x	x	x									x				
EMC Publishing																														
Creative Writing: The Whole Kit and Caboodle	$149.00	I-S	x				x	x					x		x	x									x	x	x				x
Institute for the Advancement of Philosophy for Children																														
Suki and Writing: How and Why Manual	37.00	I-S	x	x	x	x	x						x													x	x			

TABLE 2 COMMERCIAL MATERIALS LISTING (continued)

Company and Materials	Cost (Approx.)	Level (Sugg.)	Dimensions of Learning										Format		Components															
			Communication Skills	Cognitive Development	Affective Development	Logical Thinking	Critical Thinking	Divergent Production	Research Skills	Values Clarification	Group Dynamics	Creativity	Individual Instruction	Group Instruction	Kit	Workbook	Worksheets	Taskcards	Filmstrip(s)	Slides	Audio Tape(s)	Book(s)	Record(s)	Instructional Game	Specialized Equipment	Instructional Guide	Simulation	Other Visual Aids	Duplicating Masters	Transparencies
Interact																														
Claim	7.00	I-S	x	x	x	x	x	x				x	x	x	x		x									x				
Death	7.00	I-S	x	x	x	x	x	x	x				x	x	x		x									x				
Detective	7.00	I-S	x	x		x	x		x				x	x	x		x									x				
Mobility	7.00	I-S	x	x	x	x	x	x	x	x			x	x	x		x									x				
Persuasion	7.00	I-S	x	x	x	x	x	x				x	x	x	x		x									x				
Religion	7.00	I-S	x	x	x	x	x	x	x	x			x	x	x		x									x				
Right Brain/Left Brain	7.00	I-S	x	x			x	x				x	x	x	x		x									x				
Television	7.00	I-S	x	x	x	x	x	x	x	x			x	x	x		x									x				
Midwest Publications																														
Verbal Classifications	$ 13.00	I-S	x	x		x	x						x	x			x									x				
Verbal Sequences	13.00	I-S	x	x		x	x						x	x			x									x				
WFF'N Proof Learning Games Associates																														
On-Words	13.00	I-S	x	x		x								x										x	x					
The Center for the Humanities, Inc.																														
The Research Paper Made Easy: From Assignment to Completion	220.00	S	x	x			x		x				x	x	x				x								x				
Writing Skills—The Final Touch: Editing, Rewriting, and Polishing	220.00	S	x	x			x						x	x	x				x								x				
Educulture																														
Rhetoric and Critical Thinking: Clarity in Exposition	$225.00	S	x	x		x	x						x	x	x	x			x								x				
Methods of Expository Development	150.00	S	x	x		x	x						x	x	x	x			x								x				
Logic	225.00	S	x	x		x	x						x	x	x	x			x								x				
Style and Diction	188.00	S	x	x		x	x						x	x	x	x			x								x				
Special Kinds of Writing	150.00	S	x	x		x	x						x	x	x	x			x								x				

TABLE 2 COMMERCIAL MATERIALS LISTING (continued)

Column groups: **Dimensions of Learning** = Communication Skills, Cognitive Development, Affective Development, Logical Thinking, Critical Thinking, Divergent Production, Research Skills, Values Clarification, Group Dynamics, Creativity. **Format** = Individual Instruction, Group Instruction. **Components** = Kit, Workbook, Worksheets, Taskcards, Filmstrip(s), Slides, Audio Tape(s), Book(s), Record(s), Instructional Game, Specialized Equipment, Instructional Guide, Simulation, Other Visual Aids, Duplicating Masters, Transparencies.

Company and Materials	Cost (Approx.)	Level (Sugg.)	Communication Skills	Cognitive Development	Affective Development	Logical Thinking	Critical Thinking	Divergent Production	Research Skills	Values Clarification	Group Dynamics	Creativity	Individual Instruction	Group Instruction	Kit	Workbook	Worksheets	Taskcards	Filmstrip(s)	Slides	Audio Tape(s)	Book(s)	Record(s)	Instructional Game	Specialized Equipment	Instructional Guide	Simulation	Other Visual Aids	Duplicating Masters	Transparencies
MATH																														
Creative Publications																														
Attribute Games and Activities	$ 28.00	P	x	x		x							x	x	x		x							x	x	x		x		
Attribute Games and Problem Set	20.00	P	x	x		x							x	x	x									x	x	x		x		
Geoboard Activity Cards—Primary Set	20.00	P	x	x		x		x					x	x	x			x								x				
Mira Activities for Elementary School	6.00	P	x	x									x									x				x				
Cuisenaire Co. of America, Inc.																														
Relationshapes	54.00	P	x	x		x							x	x	x	x								x		x		x		
Resources for the Gifted—Elementary	$ 79.00	P	x	x		x							x	x	x	x							x	x	x	x				
Penichet Publishing Co.																														
The Geoboard—Math Lab Experiences—Book 3	3.00	P	x	x									x									x								
The Tangram—Math Lab Experiences—Book 1	3.00	P	x	x									x									x								
Tetrominoes—Math Lab Experiences—Book 2	3.00	P	x	x									x									x								
Teaching Resources Corp.																														
Attribute Games	45.00	P	x	x									x	x	x									x	x	x				
Activity Resources Co., Inc.																														
Attribute Acrobatics	$ 6.00	P-I	x	x		x		x					x				x									x				
Let's Pattern Block It	27.00	P-I	x	x		x		x					x	x			x	x							x		x				
Creative Publications																														
Code Cracker—Levels I and II	19.00	P-I	x	x									x	x	x												x				
Good Time Math Event Book	10.00	P-I	x	x									x									x				x				
Paper and Scissors Polygons	6.00	P-I	x	x		x		x					x									x								
Roddles	14.00	P-I	x			x	x						x	x										x	x	x				
Tangram Math Lab Kit	$ 40.00	P-I	x	x		x		x					x	x	x	x								x		x				
Think about It! Mathematics Problems of the Day	9.00	P-I	x			x	x	x					x	x								x				x				

TABLE 2 COMMERCIAL MATERIALS LISTING (continued)

Column groups: columns under **Dimensions of Learning** (Communication Skills → Creativity), **Format** (Individual Instruction, Group Instruction), and **Components** (Kit → Transparencies).

Company and Materials	Cost (Approx.)	Level (Sugg.)	Communication Skills	Cognitive Development	Affective Development	Logical Thinking	Critical Thinking	Divergent Production	Research Skills	Values Clarification	Group Dynamics	Creativity	Individual Instruction	Group Instruction	Kit	Workbook	Worksheets	Taskcards	Filmstrip(s)	Slides	Audio Tape(s)	Book(s)	Record(s)	Instructional Game	Specialized Equipment	Instructional Guide	Simulation	Other Visual Aids	Duplicating Masters	Transparencies
Try-a-Tile Cards	46.00	P-I		x		x	x	x					x					x									x				
What Are My Chances: Books A and B	16.00	P-I		x		x							x			x											x				
Creative Teaching Assoc.																														
Probability Lab	14.00	P-I		x		x							x	x															x	x	x
Cuisenaire Company of America, Inc.																														
Notable Numbers	6.00	P-I		x		x							x	x			x									x				
Number Triangles	6.00	P-I		x		x							x	x			x									x				x
Solve It: A Basic Approach to Problem Solving	35.00	P-I		x		x	x	x					x	x					x								x				
Wollygoggles and Other Creatures	6.00	P-I		x		x							x	x			x									x				
Disseminators of Knowledge Publishers																														
Mathematics Through Creative Thinking	4.00	P-I		x		x		x					x	x			x									x				
Educational Insights, Inc.																														
Unique Math Games	10.00	P-I		x		x							x	x			x									x				
Geo Books																														
A First Book of Space Form Making	4.00	P-I		x		x							x			x														
D.C. Heath and Co.																														
Chisanbop	58.00	P-I		x		x							x	x			x									x				
WFF'N Proof Learning Games Associates																														
On-Sets	13.00	P-I	x	x		x	x						x	x										x	x	x				
The Real Numbers Game	3.00	P-I	x	x		x	x						x	x										x	x	x				
Creative Publications																														
Aftermath: Books 1, 2, 3, and 4	$ 32.00	P-I-S		x		x	x	x					x				x									x				
Activity Resources Co., Inc.																														
Algebra in the Concrete	5.00	I		x		x							x			x										x				

TABLE 2   COMMERCIAL MATERIALS LISTING (continued)

Company and Materials	Cost (Approx.)	Level (Sugg.)	Dimensions of Learning										Format		Components															
			Communication Skills	Cognitive Development	Affective Development	Logical Thinking	Critical Thinking	Divergent Production	Research Skills	Values Clarification	Group Dynamics	Creativity	Individual Instruction	Group Instruction	Kit	Workbook	Worksheets	Taskcards	Filmstrip(s)	Slides	Audio Tape(s)	Book(s)	Record(s)	Instructional Game	Specialized Equipment	Instructional Guide	Simulation	Other Visual Aids	Duplicating Masters	Transparencies
Creative Publications																														
Adventures with Arithmetic Algebra, Book IV	6.00	I	x	x									x			x										x				
The Book of Think	6.00	I	x	x	x								x			x										x				
Creative Constructions	7.00	I	x	x	x	x			x				x			x														
Geoboard Activity Cards Intermediate Set	20.00	I	x	x		x							x		x	x		x									x				
Geometry and Visualization	$ 46.00	I	x	x	x	x							x	x											x	x	x				
Line Designs	7.00	I	x	x		x							x			x											x				
Mathemagination Book F Geometry, Measurement, and Cartesian Coordinates	6.00	I	x	x									x			x											x				
Mathematics in Science and Society	36.00	I	x	x	x	x	x						x	x					x					x	x	x				
Mira Math for Junior High School Geometry	6.00	I	x	x									x			x											x				
Cuisenaire Co. of America, Inc.																														
Resources for the Gifted— Junior High	$ 79.00	I	x	x		x							x	x	x	x								x	x	x	x			
Midwest Publications																														
Amusements in Developing Algebra Skills, Vols. I and II	14.00	I	x	x									x	x	x												x				
Learning Math Visually	13.00	I	x	x		x							x	x	x												x				
Schoolmasters Science																														
Electronic Computer	38.00	I	x	x	x	x							x			x										x	x			
Special Learning Corp.																														
Making Changes	$ 60.00	I	x	x		x							x		x	x	x	x				x				x			x	x
Sunburst Communications																														
Have I Got a Problem for You! Math Challenges	$ 85.00	I	x	x		x							x	x	x				x	x						x				
Have I Got a Problem for You! Math for Math Lovers	85.00	I	x	x		x							x	x	x		x	x								x				

TABLE 2 COMMERCIAL MATERIALS LISTING (continued)

Company and Materials	Cost (Approx.)	Level (Sugg.)	Communication Skills	Cognitive Development	Affective Development	Logical Thinking	Critical Thinking	Divergent Production	Research Skills	Values Clarification	Group Dynamics	Creativity	Individual Instruction	Group Instruction	Kit	Workbook	Worksheets	Taskcards	Filmstrip(s)	Slides	Audio Tape(s)	Book(s)	Record(s)	Instructional Game	Specialized Equipment	Instructional Guide	Simulation	Other Visual Aids	Duplicating Masters	Transparencies
Trillium Press																														
Problemoids (Grades 5 and 6 Math Enrichment)	30.00	I		x		x	x						x		x												x				
WFF'N Proof Learning Games Associates																														
Equations	13.00	I	x	x		x							x		x									x	x	x				
Tri-Nim	7.00	I	x			x							x		x									x	x	x				
Activity Resources Co., Inc.																														
Algebra in the Concrete	$ 5.00	I-S	x			x							x	x	x											x				
Quadriflex Model Book	4.00	I-S	x			x		x		x			x	x	x											x				
Creative Publications																														
Mathematical Models	18.00	I-S	x			x		x					x	x										x						
Patterns in Space	15.00	I-S	x			x		x					x	x										x		x				
Problem-Mathics: Mathematical Challenge Problems with Solution Strategies	9.00	I-S	x			x	x						x				x													
Puzzles in Space	7.00	I-S	x			x		x					x	x										x						
Statistics and Information Organization	$ 46.00	I-S	x			x	x	x	x				x	x							x			x		x				x
Tessellations	10.00	I-S	x			x		x		x			x				x									x				
Fisher Scientific Co.																														
Probability and Genetics Kit	17.00	I-S	x			x							x	x	x											x		x		
Midwest Publications																														
Amusements in Developing Geometry Skills, Vols. I-III	19.00	I-S	x	x		x	x						x				x									x				
J. Weston Walsh, Publisher																														
Discovery Problems for Better Students	$ 5.00	I-S	x			x	x	x					x				x													
Probability in Your Life	5.00	I-S	x			x		x					x				x									x				
WFF'N Proof Learning Games Associates																														
Configurations	8.00	I-S	x			x	x						x	x										x	x	x				

TABLE 2 COMMERCIAL MATERIALS LISTING (continued)

Company and Materials	Cost (Approx.)	Level (Sugg.)	Communication Skills	Cognitive Development	Affective Development	Logical Thinking	Critical Thinking	Divergent Production	Research Skills	Values Clarification	Group Dynamics	Creativity	Individual Instruction	Group Instruction	Kit	Workbook	Worksheets	Taskcards	Filmstrip(s)	Slides	Audio Tape(s)	Book(s)	Record(s)	Instructional Game	Specialized Equipment	Instructional Guide	Simulation	Other Visual Aids	Duplicating Masters	Transparencies
SCIENCE																														
Coronet																														
Science and Imagination	79.00	P	x			x	x	x					x						x	x								x	x	x
Educational Development Corp.																														
Rockets and Spaceflight	$ 3.00	P		x		x							x									x								
Sun, Moon, and Planets	3.00	P		x		x							x									x								
Things at Home	3.00	P		x		x							x									x								
Things Outdoors	3.00	P		x		x							x									x								
Educational Insights, Inc.																														
The Science Box	10.00	P	x			x	x		x				x	x	x											x				
Humanics Limited																														
Aerospace Projects for Young Children	13.00	P	x			x	x	x	x			x	x	x	x											x				
Scholastic, Inc.																														
Beginning Concepts in Science	$110.00	P	x			x	x	x	x				x						x	x								x		
Ampersand Press																														
Pollination Game	7.00	P-I	x			x							x												x	x	x				
Predator: The Food Chain Game	6.00	P-I	x			x							x												x	x	x				
Edmund Scientific Co.																														
Solar Energy Inventor's Kit	15.00	P-I	x			x	x	x	x				x	x												x	x				
Educational Insights, Inc.																														
Discovering Nature	10.00	P-I	x			x	x		x				x	x				x									x				
Elementary Science Experiments	$ 10.00	P-I	x			x	x		x				x				x	x									x				
Magnetism and Electricity	7.00	P-I	x			x	x	x	x				x				x	x									x				
Foxtail Press																														
For Thinking Rockhounds	14.00	P-I	x			x	x	x				x	x	x	x												x				
The Learning Works																														
Weather, Electricity, Environmental Investigations	9.00	P-I	x	x		x	x	x	x				x	x	x												x				

TABLE 2   COMMERCIAL MATERIALS LISTING (continued)

Company and Materials	Cost (Approx.)	Level (Sugg.)	Dimensions of Learning										Format		Components															
			Communication Skills	Cognitive Development	Affective Development	Logical Thinking	Critical Thinking	Divergent Production	Research Skills	Values Clarification	Group Dynamics	Creativity	Individual Instruction	Group Instruction	Kit	Workbook	Worksheets	Taskcards	Filmstrip(s)	Slides	Audio Tape(s)	Book(s)	Record(s)	Instructional Game	Specialized Equipment	Instructional Guide	Simulation	Other Visual Aids	Duplicating Masters	Transparencies
Activity Resources Co., Inc.																														
Climate in 3-D	4.00	I	x	x		x	x		x		x		x					x								x	x			
Ampersand Press																														
AC/DC: The Electric Circuit Game	$ 6.00	I	x			x							x											x	x	x				
Krill	6.00	I	x			x							x											x	x	x				
Carolina Biological Supply Co.																														
Food Analysis Biokit	25.00	I	x			x	x		x				x	x											x	x				
Molecules of Life Biokit	60.00	I	x			x	x		x				x	x											x	x				
Photosynthesis Biokit	35.00	I	x			x	x		x				x	x											x	x				
Seed Germination Physiology Biokit	39.00	I	x			x	x		x				x	x											x	x				
Central Scientific Co., Inc.																														
Combination Soil Test Kit	$ 22.00	I	x				x		x				x			x	x								x	x				
Human Genetics Unit	10.00	I	x			x	x		x				x									x			x	x				
Student Water Test Kit	23.00	I	x			x	x		x				x			x	x								x	x				
Task Oriented Physical Science T.O.P.S. Cards—Chemistry	38.00	I	x			x	x		x				x	x				x								x				
Task Oriented Physical Science T.O.P.S. Cards—Physics	116.00	I	x			x	x		x				x	x				x								x				
Edmund Scientific Co.																														
Aeronautics Lab	22.00	I	x			x	x		x				x	x	x										x	x				
Economy Weatherkit	35.00	I	x			x	x		x				x	x	x										x	x				
Electricity Lab Kit	$ 40.00	I	x			x	x		x				x	x											x	x				
Electronics Lab Kit	25.00	I	x			x	x		x				x	x											x	x				
Electronics Project Kit	80.00	I	x			x	x		x				x	x											x	x				
Energy Lab	40.00	I	x			x	x		x				x	x											x	x				
Educational Insights, Inc.																														
Earth Science	7.00	I	x				x		x				x	x				x								x				
The Solar System	7.00	I	x				x		x				x	x				x								x				

TABLE 2   COMMERCIAL MATERIALS LISTING (continued)

Company and Materials	Cost (Approx.)	Level (Sugg.)	Dimensions of Learning										Format		Components															
			Communication Skills	Cognitive Development	Affective Development	Logical Thinking	Critical Thinking	Divergent Production	Research Skills	Values Clarification	Group Dynamics	Creativity	Individual Instruction	Group Instruction	Kit	Workbook	Worksheets	Taskcards	Filmstrip(s)	Slides	Audio Tape(s)	Book(s)	Record(s)	Instructional Game	Specialized Equipment	Instructional Guide	Simulation	Other Visual Aids	Duplicating Masters	Transparencies
Encyclopedia Brittanica Educational Corp.																														
Collecting and Preserving Plant Specimens	$ 90.00	I	x			x	x						x	x	x				x							x				
Hand Lens and Microscope Techniques	75.00	I	x			x	x						x	x	x				x							x				
Maintaining Biological Specimens	90.00	I	x			x	x						x	x	x				x							x				
Organizing a Science Project	120.00	I	x			x	x						x	x	x				x							x				
Eye Gate Media																														
Astronomy: Unlocking the Mysteries of the Universe	81.00	I	x			x							x	x	x				x		x					x		x		
Energy: Here Today—Gone Tomorrow?	$ 68.00	I	x	x	x	x	x	x						x	x				x		x					x				
The Ocean Floor	102.00	I	x			x							x	x	x				x		x					x				
Schoolmasters Science																														
Aeronautics	24.00	I	x			x	x	x						x	x											x	x			
Death of a River Module	37.00	I	x			x	x							x	x						x					x	x			x
Electronics	18.00	I	x			x	x						x													x	x			
Super Electric Magnetic and Telecommunications Kit	27.00	I	x			x	x						x													x	x			
10-1 Electronics Kit	14.00	I	x			x	x						x													x	x			
Special Learning Corp.																														
Living Things	$ 60.00	I	x	x		x	x	x				x	x	x	x	x						x				x	x		x	
Carolina Biological Supply Co.																														
Adventures of the Mind: Space	38.00	I-S	x			x							x							x	x					x				
Chromosome Simulation Biokit	67.00	I-S	x			x	x	x					x													x	x			
Genetic Concepts Biokit	18.00	I-S	x			x	x	x					x													x	x			
Human Genetics Biokit	9.00	I-S	x			x	x	x					x													x	x			
Model Rocket Field Operations Kit	20.00	I-S	x			x	x	x					x												x	x	x			

TABLE 2   COMMERCIAL MATERIALS LISTING (continued)

Company and Materials	Cost (Approx.)	Level (Sugg.)	Dimensions of Learning										Format		Components															
			Communication Skills	Cognitive Development	Affective Development	Logical Thinking	Critical Thinking	Divergent Production	Research Skills	Values Clarification	Group Dynamics	Creativity	Individual Instruction	Group Instruction	Kit	Workbook	Worksheets	Taskcards	Filmstrip(s)	Slides	Audio Tape(s)	Book(s)	Record(s)	Instructional Game	Specialized Equipment	Instructional Guide	Simulation	Other Visual Aids	Duplicating Masters	Transparencies
The Center for the Humanities, Inc.																														
Critical Issues in Science and Society: A World to Feed	$170.00	I-S	x	x	x			x	x	x	x	x		x	x						x					x				
Ecology Sampling Methods and Field Techniques	170.00	I-S	x	x		x			x					x	x						x					x				
The Great Energy Debate	170.00	I-S	x	x	x			x	x	x	x	x		x	x						x					x				
How Do You Figure That? Ways of Problem Solving	170.00	I-S	x	x		x	x	x	x					x	x						x					x				
Nuclear Energy: Peril or Promise	170.00	I-S	x	x	x	x	x	x	x	x	x	x		x	x						x					x				
Central Scientific Co., Inc.																														
Blood Smear Study Kit	$ 10.00	I-S	x				x		x				x	x	x										x	x				
Blood Typing Kit	11.00	I-S	x				x		x				x	x	x										x	x				
Energy Changes in Chemical Reactions	42.00	I-S	x			x	x		x				x		x										x	x				
Evolution/Natural Selection Unit	27.00	I-S	x			x	x		x				x							x					x	x				
Identification of Chemical Reaction Unit	30.00	I-S	x			x	x		x				x	x	x		x								x	x				
Identification of Substance Kit	30.00	I-S	x			x	x		x				x		x										x	x				
Introduction to Biochemistry Kit	48.00	I-S	x			x	x		x				x	x	x	x									x	x				
Metabolic Rate Unit	40.00	I-S	x			x	x		x				x	x	x		x								x	x				
Rh Blood Typing Unit	$ 11.00	I-S	x				x		x				x	x	x										x	x				
Student DNA Kit	23.00	I-S	x				x		x				x	x	x	x									x	x				
Creative Learning Systems, Inc.																														
Electromechanical Kit	$110.00	I-S	x			x		x	x				x		x										x	x				
Electronics Kit	150.00	I-S	x			x		x	x				x		x										x	x				
Pneumatics Kit	160.00	I-S	x			x		x	x				x		x										x	x				
Edmund Scientific Co.																														
Fiber Optics Experiment Kit	29.00	I-S	x			x	x		x				x		x										x	x				
Educational Activities, Inc.																														
Lasers	22.00	I-S	x			x	x						x	x					x	x						x				

TABLE 2   COMMERCIAL MATERIALS LISTING (continued)

Company and Materials	Cost (Approx.)	Level (Sugg.)	Dimensions of Learning										Format		Components														
			Communication Skills	Cognitive Development	Affective Development	Logical Thinking	Critical Thinking	Divergent Production	Research Skills	Values Clarification	Group Dynamics	Creativity	Individual Instruction	Group Instruction	Kit	Workbook	Worksheets	Taskcards	Filmstrip(s)	Slides	Audio Tape(s)	Book(s)	Record(s)	Instructional Game	Specialized Equipment	Instructional Guide	Simulation	Other Visual Aids	Duplicating Masters	Transparencies
Eye Gate Media																														
Introduction to Genetics	$102.00	I-S	x	x	x	x							x	x	x				x	x						x				
Laws of Science	170.00	I-S	x			x	x						x	x	x				x	x						x				
Nuclear Radiation	102.00	I-S	x	x	x	x		x					x	x	x				x	x						x				
Fisher Scientific Co.																														
Bugley—A Genetics Experience	47.00	I-S	x		x		x						x	x	x	x									x	x		x		
Elements of Genetics	48.00	I-S	x		x		x						x	x	x	x					x					x				x
Energy and Society: Investigations in Decision Making	38.00	I-S	x	x	x	x	x	x						x		x										x				
Energy Management Game	$39.00	I-S	x	x	x	x	x	x						x									x	x	x				
Introduction to Microbiology Kit	36.00	I-S	x		x		x						x	x	x								x		x	x		x		
Natural Selection Experiment Kit	27.00	I-S	x			x	x		x				x	x											x	x				
Probability and Genetics Kit	17.00	I-S	x			x		x	x				x	x	x			x					x		x	x				
The Scientific Approach	35.00	I-S	x			x	x		x				x													x				
Solar Energy Inventor Kit	16.00	I-S	x			x		x	x				x												x	x				
Ideal School Supply Co.																														
Gomston (Ecology Simulation)	$39.00	I-S	x	x	x	x	x	x	x				x	x								x	x	x	x	x	x	x		x
Energy X (Natural Resources Simulation)	28.00	I-S	x	x	x	x	x		x	x	x		x	x								x	x	x		x		x	x	x
Interact																														
Right Brain/Left Brain	7.00	I-S	x	x			x	x		x			x	x	x										x	x				
Scholastic, Inc.																														
Human Issues in Science	385.00	I-S	x	x	x		x	x		x			x	x	x				x	x						x				
Schoolmasters Science																														
Motor Generator	14.00	I-S	x			x	x						x	x												x	x			
Radiotronics	33.00	I-S	x			x	x						x	x												x	x			
Super Electronic Thing	$27.00	I-S	x			x	x						x	x												x	x			
Telescope Astronomy	14.00	I-S	x			x	x						x	x												x	x			
Carolina Biological Supply Co.																														
Bacterial Investigation Biokit	27.00	S	x			x	x		x				x	x												x	x			

TABLE 2   COMMERCIAL MATERIALS LISTING (continued)

Company and Materials	Cost (Approx.)	Level (Sugg.)	Dimensions of Learning										Format		Components															
			Communication Skills	Cognitive Development	Affective Development	Logical Thinking	Critical Thinking	Divergent Production	Research Skills	Values Clarification	Group Dynamics	Creativity	Individual Instruction	Group Instruction	Kit	Workbook	Worksheets	Taskcards	Filmstrip(s)	Slides	Audio Tape(s)	Book(s)	Record(s)	Instructional Game	Specialized Equipment	Instructional Guide	Simulation	Other Visual Aids	Duplicating Masters	Transparencies
Drosophila Biokit	49.00	S	x			x	x		x				x		x										x	x				
Exploring the Brain: The Newest Frontier	100.00	S	x			x	x						x		x						x	x				x				
Human Chromosome Analysis Biokit	14.00	S	x			x	x		x				x		x										x	x				
Novo Enzyme Kit	$ 27.00	S	x			x	x		x				x		x										x	x				
Central Scientific Co., Inc.																														
Chemical Equilibrium Unit	28.00	S	x			x	x		x				x				x								x	x				
Environment vs. Heredity Unit	25.00	S	x			x	x		x				x	x			x								x	x				
Gel-Cels: Experimenting in Electrochemistry	33.00	S	x			x	x		x				x		x		x								x	x				
Nuclear Energy Minicourse: Introduction to Radio-activity	67.00	S	x	x	x	x	x	x	x	x	x		x		x	x	x		x						x	x				
Oxidation-Reduction Unit	$ 29.00	S	x			x	x		x				x				x								x	x				
Salt Analysis Kit	54.00	S	x			x	x		x				x		x		x								x	x				
Spectroscopic and Flame Test Unit	28.00	S	x			x	x		x				x		x		x								x	x				
Fisher Scientific Co.																														
Natural Genetic Engineering Kit	35.00	S	x			x	x		x				x		x										x	x				
SOCIAL STUDIES																														
Coronet																														
Favorite Mysteries	89.00	P-I	x	x		x	x	x					x						x											
Unsolved Mysteries	$ 89.00	P-I	x	x		x	x	x					x						x											
Educational Insights, Inc.																														
Create-a-Country	8.00	P-I	x	x			x	x			x		x	x														x		x
WFF'N Proof Learning Games Associates																														
Propaganda Game	13.00	P-I	x	x		x	x				x		x			x								x	x	x				
Interact																														
Claim	7.00	I	x	x	x	x	x	x			x		x		x		x								x	x				
Council	35.00	I	x	x		x	x	x	x	x	x		x			x									x	x				

TABLE 2 COMMERCIAL MATERIALS LISTING (continued)

Company and Materials	Cost (Approx.)	Level (Sugg.)	Communication Skills	Cognitive Development	Affective Development	Logical Thinking	Critical Thinking	Divergent Production	Research Skills	Values Clarification	Group Dynamics	Creativity	Individual Instruction	Group Instruction	Kit	Workbook	Worksheets	Taskcards	Filmstrip(s)	Slides	Audio Tape(s)	Book(s)	Record(s)	Instructional Game	Specialized Equipment	Instructional Guide	Simulation	Other Visual Aids	Duplicating Masters	Transparencies
			Dimensions of Learning										Format		Components															
Ecopolis	16.00	I	x	x	x		x	x		x	x		x			x										x	x			
Flight	17.00	I	x	x		x	x	x		x			x					x								x	x			
Locality	$ 7.00	I	x	x	x		x	x	x	x	x		x		x	x										x	x			
Mummy's Message	35.00	I	x	x	x	x	x	x		x			x		x											x	x	x		
Charles E. Merrill Publishing Co.																														
Foundations of Justice	108.00	I	x	x	x		x	x		x	x	x	x				x		x	x							x			
Science Research Associates, Inc.																														
Researchlab	190.00	I	x	x		x					x		x	x	x						x		x				x			
Simile II																														
New City Telephone Company	20.00	I	x	x		x	x	x		x			x		x		x							x	x	x	x	x	x	x
Rafa' Rafa' (A Cross Cultural Simulation)	$ 20.00	I	x	x	x	x	x			x	x		x		x								x			x	x	x	x	
Special Learning Corp.																														
Discovering History	60.00	I	x	x		x	x	x	x				x	x	x		x					x	x				x	x		
Eskimo Carving	60.00	I	x	x		x	x	x	x			x	x	x	x		x					x	x				x	x		
The Center for the Humanities, Inc.																														
Critical Issues in Science and Society: A World to Feed	170.00	I-S	x	x	x		x	x	x	x	x		x	x					x								x			
The Great Energy Debate	170.00	I-S	x	x	x		x	x	x	x	x		x	x					x								x			
EMI																														
Doomsday: The 21st Century	$ 69.00	I-S	x	x	x		x	x		x	x		x	x							x				x		x			
Ideal School Supply Co.																														
Energy X (Natural Resources Simulation)	39.00	I-S	x	x		x	x	x	x	x			x	x							x	x				x	x	x	x	
Gomston (Ecology Simulation)	28.00	I-S	x	x		x	x	x	x	x			x	x							x	x				x	x	x	x	x
Institute for the Advancement of Philosophy for Children																														
Mark and Social Inquiry Manual	37.00	I-S	x	x	x	x	x						x												x		x			
Interact																														
Death	$ 7.00	I-S	x	x	x		x	x	x	x	x		x	x	x												x	x		
Dig II	35.00	I-S	x	x		x	x	x	x		x	x	x			x											x	x		

TABLE 2 COMMERCIAL MATERIALS LISTING (continued)

Company and Materials	Cost (Approx.)	Level (Sugg.)	Communication Skills	Cognitive Development	Affective Development	Logical Thinking	Critical Thinking	Divergent Production	Research Skills	Values Clarification	Group Dynamics	Creativity	Individual Instruction	Group Instruction	Kit	Workbook	Worksheets	Taskcards	Filmstrip(s)	Slides	Audio Tape(s)	Book(s)	Record(s)	Instructional Game	Specialized Equipment	Instructional Guide	Simulation	Other Visual Aids	Duplicating Masters	Transparencies
Exchange	17.00	I-S	x	x		x	x				x		x			x	x											x	x	x
Mobility	7.00	I-S	x	x	x	x	x	x	x	x			x		x		x												x	x
Persuasion	7.00	I-S	x	x	x	x	x	x		x			x		x														x	x
Pressure	16.00	I-S	x	x		x	x	x	x	x			x			x												x	x	x
Religion	7.00	I-S	x	x	x	x	x	x	x	x			x				x												x	x
Right Brain/Left Brain	7.00	I-S	x	x			x	x			x		x		x		x												x	x
Television	$ 7.00	I-S	x	x	x	x	x	x	x	x			x		x		x												x	x
Vote	16.00	I-S	x	x	x	x	x	x	x	x			x				x												x	x
Charles E. Merrill Publishing Co.																														
In Search of Justice	180.00	I-S		x	x	x	x	x		x			x	x	x			x								x				
Simile II																														
Bafa' Bafa' (A Cross Culture Simulation)	40.00	I-S	x	x	x	x	x				x	x	x	x	x											x	x		x	x
Humanus (Futurism)	15.00	I-S	x	x	x	x	x	x			x	x	x	x	x											x	x		x	x
Napoli (National Politics)	50.00	I-S	x	x		x	x	x		x			x	x	x											x	x		x	x
Social Studies School Service																														
Global Futures Game	$ 18.00	I-S	x	x	x	x	x			x			x	x											x	x	x	x	x	x
Synergetics																														
Stones and Bones: Archeology	15.00	I-S	x	x		x	x	x	x				x	x											x				x	x
The Center for the Humanities, Inc.																														
Perspectives on Death	170.00	S	x	x	x	x	x			x	x		x						x	x			x			x				
The Science and Ethics of Population Control: An Overpopulated Earth	170.00	S	x	x	x	x	x	x	x	x			x	x					x	x			x			x				
Greenhaven Press																														
Futures Planning Games	$ 26.00	S	x	x	x	x	x			x	x		x	x													x			x
Isms Series of Opposing Viewpoints	36.00	S	x	x	x	x	x			x	x		x	x								x				x				x
Modern World Problems Series	18.00	S	x	x	x	x	x			x	x		x	x								x				x				x
Opposing Viewpoints Pamphlet Series	178.00	S	x	x	x	x	x	x		x	x		x	x								x				x				x
Opposing Viewpoints Series	120.00	S	x	x	x	x	x	x		x	x		x	x								x				x				x

TABLE 2 COMMERCIAL MATERIALS LISTING (continued)

Company and Materials	Cost (Approx.)	Level (Sugg.)	Dimensions of Learning										Format		Components																
			Communication Skills	Cognitive Development	Affective Development	Logical Thinking	Critical Thinking	Divergent Production	Research Skills	Values Clarification	Group Dynamics	Creativity	Individual Instruction	Group Instruction	Kit	Workbook	Worksheets	Taskcards	Filmstrip(s)	Slides	Audio Tape(s)	Book(s)	Record(s)	Instructional Game	Specialized Equipment	Instructional Guide	Simulation	Other Visual Aids	Duplicating Masters	Transparencies
Guidance Associates, Inc.																															
Values in a Democracy: Making Ethical Decisions	220.00	S	x	x	x		x	x		x	x		x	x					x	x						x				x
Simile II																															
Starpower (Social Groups and Power	$ 35.00	S	x	x	x	x	x	x		x	x		x	x	x											x	x	x	x	
Social Studies School Service																															
Value Questionnaires for United States History	5.00	S	x	x	x	x	x			x	x		x													x				x
MULTIDISCIPLINARY																															
Foxtail Press																															
The Dig for Dinosaurs	10.00	P	x			x	x	x				x	x	x	x											x				
Pondering Plants	14.00	P	x			x	x	x				x	x	x	x											x				
Sound Ideas: Focus on Cognition Level I	$ 13.00	P	x				x						x	x	x											x				
Sound Ideas: Focus on Cognition, Level II	13.00	P	x				x						x	x	x											x				
Sound Ideas: Focus on Convergent Production Level I	14.00	P	x				x	x					x	x	x											x				
Sound Ideas: Focus on Convergent Production Level II	14.00	P	x				x	x					x	x	x											x				
Sound Ideas: Focus on Evaluation Level I	16.00	P	x				x						x	x	x											x				
Sound Ideas: Focus on Evaluation Level II	16.00	P	x				x						x	x	x											x				
Good Apple, Inc.																															
The Cemetery Box	$ 11.00	P	x	x				x					x	x	x		x							x		x				
Addison-Wesley Publishing Co.																															
Essence I	30.00	P-I	x	x	x	x	x	x	x				x	x	x						x			x	x	x				
Essence II	50.00	P-I	x	x	x	x	x	x	x				x	x	x						x			x	x	x				
Charlotte's Web																															
Architexture: A Shelter World	11.00	P-I	x				x	x					x	x	x									x		x				
Disseminators of Knowledge, Publishers																															
Space	5.00	P-I	x	x		x	x	x	x				x	x	x											x				

TABLE 2   COMMERCIAL MATERIALS LISTING (continued)

Company and Materials	Cost (Approx.)	Level (Sugg.)	Dimensions of Learning										Format		Components															
			Communication Skills	Cognitive Development	Affective Development	Logical Thinking	Critical Thinking	Divergent Production	Research Skills	Values Clarification	Group Dynamics	Creativity	Individual Instruction	Group Instruction	Kit	Workbook	Worksheets	Taskcards	Filmstrip(s)	Slides	Audio Tape(s)	Book(s)	Record(s)	Instructional Game	Specialized Equipment	Instructional Guide	Simulation	Other Visual Aids	Duplicating Masters	Transparencies
Foxtail Press																														
For Thinking Rockhounds	$ 14.00	P-I	x			x	x	x				x	x	x	x											x				
Harcourt Brace Jovanovich																														
Expressions	60.00	P-I	x	x	x	x	x	x	x				x		x	x			x							x				
The Learning Works																														
Creative Investigations	5.00	P-I	x	x		x	x	x				x	x	x	x											x				
Mythology, Archeology, Architecture	9.00	P-I	x	x		x	x	x				x	x	x	x											x				
Structure of the Intellect Institute																														
Convergent Production Workbook—Basic	12.00	P-I	x	x		x							x			x										x				
Divergent Production Workbook—Basic	$ 12.00	P-I	x	x				x				x	x			x										x				
Evaluation Workbook—Basic	12.00	P-I	x	x		x	x						x			x										x				
California Learning Simulations																														
Game—Sim Series I	250.00	I	x	x	x	x	x	x	x		x		x		x									x	x			x		x
Charlotte's Web																														
Man Creates: Inventors	$ 12.00	I	x	x	x	x	x	x					x	x									x			x				
Creative Learning Press, Inc.																														
Mission: Possible	15.00	I	x					x	x	x			x								x					x				
Foxtail Press																														
Sound Ideas: Focus on Cognition Level III	13.00	I	x			x							x	x		x										x				
Sound Ideas: Focus on Cognition Level IV	13.00	I	x			x							x	x		x										x				
Sound Ideas: Focus on Convergent Production Level III	14.00	I	x			x	x						x	x		x										x				
Sound Ideas: Focus on Convergent Production Level IV	14.00	I	x			x	x						x	x		x										x				
Sound Ideas: Focus on Evaluation Level III	$ 16.00	I	x				x						x	x		x										x				
Sound Ideas: Focus on Evaluation Level IV	16.00	I	x				x						x	x		x										x				

TABLE 2 COMMERCIAL MATERIALS LISTING (continued)

Company and Materials	Cost (Approx.)	Level (Sugg.)	Dimensions of Learning										Format		Components															
			Communication Skills	Cognitive Development	Affective Development	Logical Thinking	Critical Thinking	Divergent Production	Research Skills	Values Clarification	Group Dynamics	Creativity	Individual Instruction	Group Instruction	Kit	Workbook	Worksheets	Taskcards	Filmstrip(s)	Slides	Audio Tape(s)	Book(s)	Record(s)	Instructional Game	Specialized Equipment	Instructional Guide	Simulation	Other Visual Aids	Duplicating Masters	Transparencies
Structure of the Intellect Institute																														
Convergent Production Workbook—Advanced	12.00	I-S	x	x		x							x			x										x				
Divergent Production Workbook—Advanced	12.00	I-S	x	x				x					x			x										x				
Evaluation Workbook—Advanced	12.00	I-S	x	x		x	x						x			x										x				
Creative Learning Systems, Inc.																														
CLS Communication Kit	50.00	S	x	x	x			x					x	x								x			x	x				
CREATIVITY																														
Creative Publications																														
Think! Draw! Write! Levels I and II	12.00	P	x	x			x	x				x	x														x				x
Creative Teaching Press, Inc.																														
Desk Top Story Starters	$ 5.00	P	x					x					x		x	x										x				x
Make-Believe Story Starters	5.00	P	x					x					x		x	x										x				x
Super Size Story Starters	5.00	P	x					x					x		x	x										x				x
Curriculum Associates, Inc.																														
Elaborative Thinking Kit—Primary	9.00	P	x	x			x						x		x	x	x				x					x				x
Story Starters—Primary	12.00	P	x					x					x		x	x						x				x				
Disseminators of Knowledge, Publishers																														
Learning Through Creative Thinking	4.00	P	x					x					x		x	x	x									x				
Educational Insights, Inc.																														
Adventure	$ 6.00	P	x					x					x		x	x										x				x
Adventure Island	6.00	P	x					x					x		x	x										x				x
Apples to Watermelon	6.00	P	x					x					x		x	x										x				x
Artichokes to Zucchini	6.00	P	x					x					x		x	x										x				x
Fantasy	6.00	P	x					x					x		x	x										x				x
Magic	6.00	P	x					x					x		x	x										x				x
Story Sparkers	7.00	P	x					x					x		x	x						x				x				

TABLE 2   COMMERCIAL MATERIALS LISTING (continued)

Company and Materials	Cost (Approx.)	Level (Sugg.)	Dimensions of Learning										Format		Components															
			Communication Skills	Cognitive Development	Affective Development	Logical Thinking	Critical Thinking	Divergent Production	Research Skills	Values Clarification	Group Dynamics	Creativity	Individual Instruction	Group Instruction	Kit	Workbook	Worksheets	Taskcards	Filmstrip(s)	Slides	Audio Tape(s)	Book(s)	Record(s)	Instructional Game	Specialized Equipment	Instructional Guide	Simulation	Other Visual Aids	Duplicating Masters	Transparencies
Welcome to Spook House	6.00	P	x					x				x	x	x												x				x
The Wild and Woolly West	6.00	P	x					x				x	x	x												x				x
Foxtail Press																													
Art and Perception	$ 10.00	P	x					x				x	x	x		x										x				
Picture This!	10.00	P	x					x				x	x	x		x										x				
Sound Ideas: Focus on Divergent Production Level I	16.00	P	x					x				x	x	x		x										x				
Sound Ideas: Focus on Divergent Production Level II	16.00	P	x					x				x	x	x		x										x				
Good Apple, Inc.																													
Creative Writing in Action	6.00	P	x					x				x	x	x		x										x				
Flights of Fantasy	14.00	P	x	x				x			x	x	x	x		x								x		x				
Future Think	$ 6.00	P	x	x		x	x	x				x	x	x		x										x				
The Good Apple Creative Writing Book	8.00	P	x					x				x	x	x		x										x				
Hippogriff Feathers	8.00	P	x	x				x			x	x	x	x		x										x				
If I Were a Road	6.00	P	x					x				x	x	x		x										x				
If I Were a Table	6.00	P	x					x				x	x	x		x										x				
Sprouts	10.00	P	x					x				x	x	x		x										x				
Sunflowering	8.00	P	x	x		x	x	x				x	x	x		x										x				
The Unconventional Invention Book	9.00	P	x					x	x			x	x	x		x										x				
Harper & Row Publishers, Inc.																													
New Directions in Creativity: Mark A	$ 24.00	P	x					x				x	x	x												x				x
New Directions in Creativity: Mark B	24.00	P	x					x				x	x	x												x				x
Hayes School Publishing Co., Inc.																													
Tampering with Tall Tales	4.00	P	x					x				x	x	x												x				x
Milliken Publishing Co.																													
Creative Expression	10.00	P	x				x					x	x	x												x			x	x
Creative Language Projects	15.00	P	x				x					x	x	x												x				x
Creative Writing	10.00	P	x				x					x	x	x												x			x	x

TABLE 2   COMMERCIAL MATERIALS LISTING (continued)

Company and Materials	Cost (Approx.)	Level (Sugg.)	Dimensions of Learning										Format		Components															
			Communication Skills	Cognitive Development	Affective Development	Logical Thinking	Critical Thinking	Divergent Production	Research Skills	Values Clarification	Group Dynamics	Creativity	Individual Instruction	Group Instruction	Kit	Workbook	Worksheets	Taskcards	Filmstrip(s)	Slides	Audio Tape(s)	Book(s)	Record(s)	Instructional Game	Specialized Equipment	Instructional Guide	Simulation	Other Visual Aids	Duplicating Masters	Transparencies
Penichet Publishing Co.																														
Starting Your Stories Activity Cards	$ 5.00	P	x					x					x	x				x								x				
Prentice-Hall Media																														
First Experiences in Creative Writing	75.00	P	x	x				x					x						x		x					x				
Frank Schaeffer Publications, Inc.																														
Creative Writing Activity Cards	6.00	P	x					x					x	x				x								x				
Troll Associates																														
Getting Ready to Write Creatively	120.00	P	x	x				x					x						x	x						x				
You Decide/Open-Ended Tales	$120.00	P	x	x				x					x						x	x						x				
Activity Resources Co., Inc.																														
Attribute Acrobatics	6.00	P-I	x			x		x					x	x			x									x				
Curriculum Associates, Inc.																														
Story Starters—Intermediate	12.00	P-I	x					x					x	x				x								x				
Disseminators of Knowledge, Publishers																														
Imagination Express	4.00	P-I	x				x	x					x	x	x													x		x
Mathematics through Creative Thinking	4.00	P-I	x			x		x					x	x	x		x									x				
Educational Insights, Inc.																														
More Write On	$ 7.00	P-I	x					x					x	x	x		x													
Foxtail Press																														
The Art of Perceiving Problems	12.00	P-I		x		x	x	x					x	x			x									x				
The Art of Resolving Problems	12.00	P-I		x		x	x	x					x	x			x									x				
Good Apple, Inc.																														
Connecting Rainbows	8.00	P-I	x		x	x	x	x					x	x			x									x				
I Believe in Unicorns	8.00	P-I	x		x		x	x					x	x			x									x				
Mighty Myth	10.00	P-I	x	x	x		x	x	x				x	x			x									x				

TABLE 2   COMMERCIAL MATERIALS LISTING (continued)

Company and Materials	Cost (Approx.)	Level (Sugg.)	Communication Skills	Cognitive Development	Affective Development	Logical Thinking	Critical Thinking	Divergent Production	Research Skills	Values Clarification	Group Dynamics	Creativity	Individual Instruction	Group Instruction	Kit	Workbook	Worksheets	Taskcards	Filmstrip(s)	Slides	Audio Tape(s)	Book(s)	Record(s)	Instructional Game	Specialized Equipment	Instructional Guide	Simulation	Other Visual Aids	Duplicating Masters	Transparencies
Wonderful Word Games	10.00	P-I	x					x				x	x	x			x									x				
Harper & Row Publishers, Inc.																														
Making It Strange: Books 1, 2, 3, and 4	$ 20.00	P-I	x					x				x	x	x			x									x				
Milliken Publishing Co.																														
Creative Language Projects	15.00	P-I	x					x				x	x	x												x			x	
Creative Writing Grades 4-6	5.00	P-I	x					x				x	x	x												x			x	x
Creative Writing Grades 6-8	5.00	P-I	x					x				x	x	x												x			x	x
Xerox Education Publications																														
Imagine and Write Program	7.00	P-I	x					x				x	x	x	x															
Creative Learning Systems, Inc.																														
Creative Cue Cards	$ 35.00	I	x			x	x	x				x	x		x			x						x		x				
Junkyard Treasures	13.00	I	x	x				x				x	x	x	x										x	x				
Things That Go Bump in the Night	13.00	I	x	x				x				x	x	x	x										x	x				
Creative Publications																														
Creative Constructions	7.00	I		x		x	x	x				x	x								x									
Line Designs	7.00	I		x		x		x				x	x								x									
Creative Teaching Press, Inc.																														
Bright Ideas	7.00	I	x	x		x	x	x				x	x	x								x								
Curriculum Associates, Inc.																														
Elaborative Thinking— Intermediate	$ 9.00	I	x	x				x				x	x	x	x				x							x		x		
Encyclopedia Brittanica Educational Corp.																														
Open Box: Ideas for Creative Expression	67.00	I	x					x				x	x	x	x							x	x	x		x	x			
Eye Gate Media																														
Creative Thoughts	68.00	I	x		x	x	x	x				x		x								x	x			x				
Foxtail Press																														
The Inventive "I": Imagery to Insight	14.00	I		x				x				x	x	x	x											x				
The Inventive "I": Imagination to Illumination	$ 14.00	I		x				x				x	x	x	x											x				

TABLE 2   COMMERCIAL MATERIALS LISTING (continued)

Company and Materials	Cost (Approx.)	Level (Sugg.)	Communication Skills	Cognitive Development	Affective Development	Logical Thinking	Critical Thinking	Divergent Production	Research Skills	Values Clarification	Group Dynamics	Creativity	Individual Instruction	Group Instruction	Kit	Workbook	Worksheets	Taskcards	Filmstrip(s)	Slides	Audio Tape(s)	Book(s)	Record(s)	Instructional Game	Specialized Equipment	Instructional Guide	Simulation	Other Visual Aids	Duplicating Masters	Transparencies
Sound Ideas: Focus on Divergent Production Level III	16.00	I	x					x					x		x	x										x				
Sound Ideas: Focus on Divergent Production Level IV	16.00	I	x					x					x		x	x										x				
Harper & Row Publishers, Inc.																														
New Directions in Creativity: Mark 1	24.00	I	x					x					x		x	x										x				x
New Directions in Creativity: Mark 2	$ 24.00	I	x					x					x		x	x										x				x
New Directions in Creativity: Mark 3	24.00	I	x					x					x		x	x										x				x
Interact																														
Patterns: The How to Write a Poem Book	16.00	I	x	x	x		x	x				x	x											x		x				
Sources	22.00	I	x	x	x		x	x				x	x				x									x				
Penichet Publishing Co.																														
Imagination and Language (Creative Writing Experiences in the Imaginative Use of Language)	8.00	I	x	x				x					x				x									x				
Dale Seymour Publications																														
Challenge Boxes: 50 Projects in Creative Thinking	$ 10.00	I	x	x				x					x				x									x				
Mind Event	7.00	I	x	x		x		x					x				x									x				
Sunburst Communications																														
Creative Problem Solving: Planning New Worlds	$ 85.00	I	x	x			x	x					x				x				x	x	x			x				
Xerox Education Publications																														
Mindgame: Experiences in Creative Writing	2.00	I	x	x				x					x		x	x									x				
Argus Communications																														
Take the Road to Creativity and Get Off Your Dead End	35.00	I-S	x		x		x	x	x	x			x	x							x	x	x			x		x		

TABLE 2 COMMERCIAL MATERIALS LISTING (continued)

Company and Materials	Cost (Approx.)	Level (Sugg.)	Dimensions of Learning										Format		Components															
			Communication Skills	Cognitive Development	Affective Development	Logical Thinking	Critical Thinking	Divergent Production	Research Skills	Values Clarification	Group Dynamics	Creativity	Individual Instruction	Group Instruction	Kit	Workbook	Worksheets	Taskcards	Filmstrip(s)	Slides	Audio Tape(s)	Book(s)	Record(s)	Instructional Game	Specialized Equipment	Instructional Guide	Simulation	Other Visual Aids	Duplicating Masters	Transparencies
The Center for the Humanities, Inc.																															
Creative Writing: Imagination and Self-Expression	220.00	I-S	x	x	x	x			x	x			x	x	x				x									x		
Learning Seed Company																															
Creativity Kit: Learn Creative Thinking	$ 69.00	I-S	x	x		x				x			x						x	x	x							x		
Sunburst Communications																															
Problem Solving: Using Your Head Creatively	159.00	I-S	x	x		x	x	x		x			x	x	x					x	x							x		
DEBATE																															
Creative Learning Systems, Inc.																															
Pros and Cons: Energy and the Environment	20.00	S	x		x	x	x	x		x			x																x	x
Pros and Cons: Technoconsequences	20.00	S	x		x	x	x	x		x			x																x	x
Pros and Cons: Timely Topics	$ 20.00	S	x		x	x	x	x		x			x			x													x	x
FUTURISM																															
Educational Development Corp.																															
Computers	4.00	P-I	x			x	x						x	x								x									
Future Cities	4.00	P-I	x			x	x						x	x								x									
Robots	4.00	P-I	x			x	x						x	x								x									
Star Travel	4.00	P-I	x			x	x						x	x								x									
Educational Insights, Inc.																															
World of the Future: The World in the 21st Century	$ 14.00	I	x	x	x	x	x						x	x					x									x		
Interact																															
Cope	16.00	I	x	x	x	x	x			x	x	x	x			x													x	x
Galaxy	40.00	I	x	x		x	x	x		x			x				x												x	x
Sunburst Communications																															
Creative Problem Solving: Planning New Worlds	85.00	I	x	x		x	x			x			x	x	x					x	x							x		

TABLE 2   COMMERCIAL MATERIALS LISTING (continued)

Company and Materials	Cost (Approx.)	Level (Sugg.)	Dimensions of Learning										Format		Components													
			Communication Skills	Cognitive Development	Affective Development	Logical Thinking	Critical Thinking	Divergent Production	Research Skills	Values Clarification	Group Dynamics	Creativity	Individual Instruction	Group Instruction	Kit	Workbook	Worksheets	Taskcards	Filmstrip(s)	Slides	Audio Tape(s)	Record(s)	Instructional Game	Specialized Equipment	Instructional Guide	Simulation	Other Visual Aids	Duplicating Masters	Transparencies
The Center for the Humanities, Inc.																													
An Inquiry into the Future of Mankind: Designing Tomorrow Today	170.00	I-S	x	x	x		x	x	x	x	x		x	x							x				x				
Critical Issues in Science and Society: A World to Feed	$170.00	I-S	x	x	x		x	x	x	x	x		x	x							x				x				
Critical Issues in Science and Society: The Great Energy Debate	170.00	I-S	x	x	x		x	x	x	x	x		x	x							x				x				
Toward the Year 2000: Can We Survive the Future?	170.00	I-S	x	x	x		x	x	x	x	x		x	x	x						x				x				
Creative Learning Systems, Inc.																													
Future-Ed	18.00	I-S	x	x	x	x	x	x			x	x	x	x									x		x	x	x	x	
EMI																													
Doomsday: The 21st Century	$ 69.00	I-S	x	x	x		x	x		x	x		x	x					x				x		x				
Global Futures Game	18.00	I-S	x	x	x		x	x			x		x										x		x				
The World to Come: Exploring the Future	129.00	I-S		x	x		x	x					x	x					x	x					x				
2000 A.D.	66.00	I-S	x	x			x	x		x			x	x	x	x	x	x	x		x	x			x				x
Simile II																													
Humans	15.00	I-S	x	x	x	x	x	x			x	x	x	x									x		x	x	x	x	
Social Studies School Service																													
Global Futures Game	18.00	I-S	x	x	x	x	x	x		x			x	x									x	x	x	x	x	x	
Synergetics																													
Grokking into the Future	$ 20.00	I-S	x	x		x	x	x	x				x										x		x	x			
Greenhaven Press																													
Future Planning Games	26.00	S	x	x	x		x	x		x	x		x	x									x		x				
Interact																													
Clone	23.00	S	x	x	x		x	x		x	x		x				x								x	x	x		
Utopia	17.00	S	x	x	x		x	x		x	x		x				x								x	x	x		
Social Studies School Service																													
Making Changes: A Futures Oriented Course	69.00	S	x	x	x	x	x			x	x		x		x	x											x		x

TABLE 2 COMMERCIAL MATERIALS LISTING (continued)

Company and Materials	Cost (Approx.)	Level (Sugg.)	Communication Skills	Cognitive Development	Affective Development	Logical Thinking	Critical Thinking	Divergent Production	Research Skills	Values Clarification	Group Dynamics	Creativity	Individual Instruction	Group Instruction	Kit	Workbook	Worksheets	Taskcards	Filmstrip(s)	Slides	Audio Tape(s)	Book(s)	Record(s)	Instructional Game	Specialized Equipment	Instructional Guide	Simulation	Other Visual Aids	Duplicating Masters	Transparencies
The World to Come. Exploring the Future	129.00	S		x	x	x	x	x			x		x						x		x					x				
Sunburst Communications																														
Encounters with Tomorrow: Science Fiction and Human Values	179.00	S	x	x	x	x		x	x				x	x					x		x					x				
Forecasting the Future: Can We Make Tomorrow Work?	179.00	S	x	x	x	x	x	x	x				x	x					x		x					x				
GROUP DYNAMICS																														
Disseminators of Knowledge, Publishers																														
Effective Communication: A Handbook of Discussion Skills	3.00	P-I	x		x		x			x	x	x	x	x			x									x				
Creative Learning Systems, Inc.																														
Dilemma	36.00	I-S	x		x		x	x		x	x		x	x										x	x	x	x			
Priority	$ 18.00	I-S	x		x		x	x		x	x		x	x										x		x	x	x			
LEADERSHIP																														
Listos Publications																														
Leadership Series	30.00	P	x	x	x		x	x		x	x	x	x	x								x				x				
Leadership Series	30.00	I	x	x	x		x	x		x	x	x	x	x								x				x				
Argus Communications																														
If I'm in Charge Here, Why Is Everybody Laughing?	35.00	I-S	x		x		x	x		x	x		x									x		x	x	x		x		x
Listos Publications																														
Leadership Series	$ 36.00	S	x	x	x		x	x		x	x	x	x	x								x				x				
LOGIC, CRITICAL THINKING, AND PROBLEM SOLVING																														
Ann Arbor Publishers, Inc.																														
Critical Reading Primers: Workbooks A, B, C, and D	17.00	P		x		x							x			x										x				
Benefic Press																														
Primary Thinking Box	174.00	P	x	x		x	x	x					x			x	x	x	x	x						x		x	x	x

TABLE 2 COMMERCIAL MATERIALS LISTING (continued)

Column groups: **Dimensions of Learning** = Communication Skills, Cognitive Development, Affective Development, Logical Thinking, Critical Thinking, Divergent Production, Research Skills, Values Clarification, Group Dynamics, Creativity; **Format** = Individual Instruction, Group Instruction; **Components** = Kit, Workbook, Worksheets, Taskcards, Filmstrip(s), Slides, Audio Tape(s), Book(s), Record(s), Instructional Game, Specialized Equipment, Instructional Guide, Simulation, Other Visual Aids, Duplicating Masters, Transparencies.

Company and Materials	Cost (Approx.)	Level (Sugg.)	Communication Skills	Cognitive Development	Affective Development	Logical Thinking	Critical Thinking	Divergent Production	Research Skills	Values Clarification	Group Dynamics	Creativity	Individual Instruction	Group Instruction	Kit	Workbook	Worksheets	Taskcards	Filmstrip(s)	Slides	Audio Tape(s)	Book(s)	Record(s)	Instructional Game	Specialized Equipment	Instructional Guide	Simulation	Other Visual Aids	Duplicating Masters	Transparencies
Creative Publications																														
Attribute Games and Activities	$ 28.00	P	x			x	x						x	x	x		x							x	x	x	x			
Attribute Games and Problems Set	20.00	P	x			x	x						x	x	x		x							x	x	x	x			
Eye Gate Media																														
Thinking Clearly: Strategies	102.00	P	x			x	x	x					x	x	x				x		x					x					
Institute for the Advancement of Philosophy for Children																														
Kio and Gus and Wondering at the World Manual	37.00	P	x	x	x	x	x							x								x				x				
Penichet Publishing Co.																														
The Tangram-Math Lab Experiences Book 1	$ 3.00	P	x			x							x		x																
Frank Schaeffer Publications, Inc.																														
Fact and Opinion	5.00	P	x			x	x						x	x														x		x
Science Research Associates, Inc.																														
Thinklab Junior	150.00	P	x			x	x	x					x					x						x	x					
Teaching Resources Corp.																														
Attribute Games	45.00	P	x			x							x	x	x									x	x	x				
Troll Associates																														
Thinking Skills	$120.00	P	x			x	x							x					x		x					x				
Academic Therapy Publications																														
Cognitive Challenge Cards	6.00	P-I	x			x	x						x			x		x								x				
Benefic Press																														
Thinking Box I	199.00	P-I	x	x		x	x	x	x				x	x	x	x	x	x	x					x	x	x		x	x	
Coronet																														
Favorite Mysteries	89.00	P-I	x	x		x	x	x						x					x											
Unsolved Mysteries	89.00	P-I	x	x		x	x	x						x					x											
Creative Publications																														
Tangram-Math Lab Kit	40.00	P-I	x			x		x						x	x	x									x	x				
Creative Teaching Associates																														
Brain Drain, Books A and B	$ 5.00	P-I	x			x	x						x			x														x
Probability Lab	14.00	P-I	x			x							x	x			x											x	x	x

TABLE 2   COMMERCIAL MATERIALS LISTING (continued)

Company and Materials	Cost (Approx.)	Level (Sugg.)	Dimensions of Learning										Format		Components																
			Communication Skills	Cognitive Development	Affective Development	Logical Thinking	Critical Thinking	Divergent Production	Research Skills	Values Clarification	Group Dynamics	Creativity	Individual Instruction	Group Instruction	Kit	Workbook	Worksheets	Taskcards	Filmstrip(s)	Slides	Audio Tape(s)	Book(s)	Record(s)	Instructional Game	Specialized Equipment	Instructional Guide	Simulation	Other Visual Aids	Duplicating Masters	Transparencies
Disseminators of Knowledge, Publishers																															
Hometown U.S. A Community of Logic	5.00	P-I	x			x	x						x	x		x								x		x				
Who Owns the Unicorn? And Other Exercises in Logic	5.00	P-I	x			x	x						x			x								x		x				
Educational Development Corp.																															
Brain Puzzles	3.00	P-I	x			x							x	x										x							
Number Puzzles	$ 3.00	P-I	x			x							x	x										x							
Picture Puzzles	3.00	P-I	x			x							x	x										x							
Eye Gate Media																															
Fundamentals of Thinking	115.00	P-I	x	x		x	x						x	x	x						x						x				
Foxtail Press																															
The Art of Perceiving Problems	12.00	P-I	x			x	x	x		x			x	x		x										x				
The Art of Resolving Problems	12.00	P-I	x			x	x	x		x			x	x		x										x				
Detecting and Deducing	11.00	P-I	x			x	x	x					x	x		x										x				
Institute for the Advancement of Philosophy for Children																															
Pixie and Looking for Meaning Manual	$ 37.00	P-I	x	x	x	x	x							x									x			x				
The Learning Works																															
Strain Your Brain	5.00	P-I	x	x		x	x	x		x			x	x		x										x				
Think Big!	7.00	P-I	x	x		x	x	x		x			x	x		x										x				
Charles E. Merrill Publishing Co.																															
The Productive Thinking Program	198.00	P-I	x	x		x	x	x			x	x	x	x	x	x										x			x	x
Midwest Publications																															
Amusements in Developing Thinking and Survival Skills	$ 4.00	P-I	x			x	x						x	x		x										x				
Basic Thinking Skills	48.00	P-I	x			x	x						x	x		x										x				
Figural Sequences	12.00	P-I	x			x	x						x	x		x										x				
Logic in Easy Steps	63.00	P-I	x			x	x						x	x		x										x				
Visual Logic	20.00	P-I	x			x	x						x	x		x										x				

TABLE 2   COMMERCIAL MATERIALS LISTING (continued)

Column groups: **Dimensions of Learning** (Communication Skills … Creativity); **Format** (Individual Instruction, Group Instruction); **Components** (Kit … Transparencies).

Company and Materials	Cost (Approx.)	Level (Sugg.)	Communication Skills	Cognitive Development	Affective Development	Logical Thinking	Critical Thinking	Divergent Production	Research Skills	Values Clarification	Group Dynamics	Creativity	Individual Instruction	Group Instruction	Kit	Workbook	Worksheets	Taskcards	Filmstrip(s)	Slides	Audio Tape(s)	Book(s)	Record(s)	Instructional Game	Specialized Equipment	Instructional Guide	Simulation	Other Visual Aids	Duplicating Masters	Transparencies
Pitman Learning, Inc.																														
Logic, Anyone?	$ 10.00	P-I	x			x							x	x												x			x	
Mind Stretchers	10.00	P-I	x			x							x	x			x									x				
Science Research Associates, Inc.																														
Thinklab	110.00	P-I	x	x		x	x	x					x	x	x				x							x	x			
Dale Seymour Publications																														
Favorite Problems	8.00	P-I	x			x	x	x					x											x		x				
Problem of the Week	13.00	P-I	x			x	x	x					x											x		x				
Super Problems	8.00	P-I	x			x	x	x					x											x		x				
Visual Thinking Cards Elementary Set	$ 20.00	P-I	x			x	x						x				x								x				
Stallard Press																														
Thinking Skills Task Cards	$ 27.00	P-I	x			x	x	x			x		x				x								x				
WFF'N Proof Learning Games Associates																														
Propaganda Game	13.00	P-I	x	x		x	x			x			x	x										x	x	x				
Tac-Tickle	2.00	P-I	x			x	x						x	x										x	x	x				
WFF	3.00	P-I	x	x		x	x						x	x										x	x	x				
B.L. Winch and Associates																														
Thinking Skills Taskcards	35.00	P-I	x	x		x	x	x					x				x								x				
Midwest Publications																														
Deductive Thinking Skills (MindBenders)	52.00	P-I-S				x	x	x					x	x		x											x		
Inductive Thinking Skills	44.00	P-I-S				x	x	x					x	x		x											x		
Ann Arbor Publishers, Inc.																														
Critical Reading Series: Books A, B, C, and D	22.00	I	x			x							x			x											x		
Benefic Press																														
Thinking Box II	$177.00	I	x	x		x	x	x	x				x	x	x				x	x	x	x	x			x			
Institute for the Advancement of Philosophy for Children																														
Harry Stottlemeir's Discovery and Philosophical Inquiry Manual	37.00	I	x	x	x	x	x						x											x		x				

TABLE 2   COMMERCIAL MATERIALS LISTING (continued)

Company and Materials	Cost (Approx.)	Level (Sugg.)	Communication Skills	Cognitive Development	Affective Development	Logical Thinking	Critical Thinking	Divergent Production	Research Skills	Values Clarification	Group Dynamics	Creativity	Individual Instruction	Group Instruction	Kit	Workbook	Worksheets	Taskcards	Filmstrip(s)	Slides	Audio Tape(s)	Book(s)	Record(s)	Instructional Game	Specialized Equipment	Instructional Guide	Simulation	Other Visual Aids	Duplicating Masters	Transparencies
Interact																														
Code	11.00	I	x	x		x	x	x			x	x	x		x	x	x									x	x			
Little, Brown and Co.																														
The Book of Think	6.00	I		x		x	x				x	x										x				x				
Midwest Publications																														
Word Benders	$ 13.00	I	x	x		x	x						x	x		x										x				
Society for Visual Education, Inc.																														
Sherlock Holmes Cliffhangers	120.00	I	x	x		x	x	x						x					x		x					x				x
Sherlock Holmes Spellbinders	120.00	I	x	x		x	x	x						x					x		x					x				x
Sunburst Communications																														
Creative Problem Solving: Planning New Worlds	85.00	I	x	x		x	x					x	x	x	x	x										x				
Sunburst Communications																														
Propoganda: What Can You Believe?	$ 85.00	I	x	x	x	x	x	x			x		x	x			x								x	x				x
B.L. Winch and Associates																														
Soar	$ 14.00	I	x	x		x	x	x					x			x										x				
The Center for the Humanities, Inc.																														
Clear Thinking: How to Improve Your Reasoning Skills	170.00	I-S	x	x		x	x	x		x			x			x									x		x				
Effective Thinking: Ways of Problem Solving	220.00	I-S	x	x		x	x	x	x	x			x			x									x		x				
How Do You Figure That? Ways of Problem Solving	170.00	I-S	x	x		x	x			x			x												x		x				
Creative Learning Systems, Inc.																														
Problems! Problems! Problems!	$ 11.00	I-S	x	x		x	x	x			x	x	x												x		x				
Creative Publications																														
Problem-mathics: Mathematical Challenge Problems with Solution Strategies	$ 9.00	I-S		x		x	x						x			x										x				

TABLE 2   COMMERCIAL MATERIALS LISTING (continued)

Company and Materials	Cost (Approx.)	Level (Sugg.)	Dimensions of Learning										Format		Components														
			Communication Skills	Cognitive Development	Affective Development	Logical Thinking	Critical Thinking	Divergent Production	Research Skills	Values Clarification	Group Dynamics	Creativity	Individual Instruction	Group Instruction	Kit	Workbook	Worksheets	Taskcards	Filmstrip(s)	Slides	Audio Tape(s)	Book(s)	Record(s)	Instructional Game	Specialized Equipment	Instructional Guide	Simulation	Other Visual Aids	Duplicating Masters	Transparencies
Successful Problem Solving Techniques	10.00	I-S	x			x	x						x											x		x				
Educulture																														
Rhetoric and Critical Thinking: Logic	225.00	I-S	x	x		x	x						x	x	x	x					x	x				x				
Foxtail Press																														
A-Way with Problems	11.00	I-S		x		x	x	x					x		x	x	x									x				
The Discovery	8.00	I-S		x		x	x	x					x		x	x	x									x				
Innovative Sciences, Inc.																														
Strategic Reasoning Kit	$298.00	I-S	x	x		x	x	x					x	x	x	x					x			x		x				
Institute for the Advancement of Philosophy For Children																														
Lisa and Ethical Inquiry Manual	27.00	I-S	x	x	x	x	x							x								x				x				
Mark and Social Inquiry Manual	37.00	I-S	x	x	x	x	x							x								x				x				
Suki and Writing: How and Why Manual	37.00	I-S	x	x	x	x	x							x								x				x				
Interact																														
Detective	7.00	I-S	x	x		x	x	x					x	x	x	x													x	x
Midwest Publications																														
Brain Stretchers, Vol. I and II	$ 13.00	I-S		x		x	x						x	x		x										x				
Classroom Quickies	12.00	I-S		x		x	x						x	x		x										x				
Critical Thinking, Book I	13.00	I-S		x		x	x						x	x		x										x				
Figural Analogies	12.00	I-S		x		x	x						x	x		x										x				
Figural Classifications	13.00	I-S		x		x	x						x	x		x										x				
Figural Similarities	17.00	I-S		x		x	x						x	x		x										x				
Syllogisms	12.00	I-S		x		x	x						x	x		x										x				
Verbal Classifications	13.00	I-S	x	x		x	x						x	x		x										x				
Verbal Sequences	13.00	I-S	x	x		x	x						x	x		x										x				
Science Research Associates, Inc.																														
Thinklab 2	140.00	I-S	x	x		x	x	x					x		x	x	x							x		x	x	x		
Dale Seymour Publications																														
Visual Thinking Cards Secondary Set	$ 20.00	I-S		x		x	x						x				x								x				

TABLE 2 COMMERCIAL MATERIALS LISTING (continued)

Company and Materials	Cost (Approx.)	Level (Sugg.)	Dimensions of Learning										Format		Components															
			Communication Skills	Cognitive Development	Affective Development	Logical Thinking	Critical Thinking	Divergent Production	Research Skills	Values Clarification	Group Dynamics	Creativity	Individual Instruction	Group Instruction	Kit	Workbook	Worksheets	Taskcards	Filmstrip(s)	Slides	Audio Tape(s)	Book(s)	Record(s)	Instructional Game	Specialized Equipment	Instructional Guide	Simulation	Other Visual Aids	Duplicating Masters	Transparencies
Stallard Press																														
Recognizing and Developing Higher Thinking Skills	23.00	I-S	x			x	x						x			x	x									x				
Sunburst Communications																														
Problem Solving: Using Your Head Creatively	159.00	I-S	x	x		x	x	x				x	x	x	x	x	x									x				
Globe Book Company, Inc.																														
Making Sense: Exploring Semantics and Critical Thinking	6.00	S	x	x		x	x						x	x								x				x				
Innovative Sciences, Inc.																														
Analytical Reading and Reasoning	18.00	S	x	x		x	x	x					x									x								
Midwest Publications																														
Critical Thinking, Book II	17.00	S	x	x		x	x						x	x		x													x
J. Weston Walsh, Publisher																														
Discovery Problems for Better Students	5.00	I-S	x			x	x		x				x				x													
WFF'N Proof Learning Games Associates																														
Queries and Theories	16.00	I-S	x	x		x	x		x					x	x									x	x	x				
WFF'N Proof	16.00	I-S	x	x		x	x							x	x									x	x	x				
RESEARCH SKILLS																														
Sunburst Communications																														
Using Reference Books	$ 85.00	P	x	x					x				x	x	x				x	x				x	x	x				
Troll Associates																														
Look It Up: How to Get Information	$ 80.00	P	x						x				x								x					x				
Coronet																														
Myth, Magic, and Mystery: Sets I, II, and III	89.00	P-I	x	x		x	x	x	x				x								x									

TABLE 2 COMMERCIAL MATERIALS LISTING (continued)

Company and Materials	Cost (Approx.)	Level (Sugg.)	Communication Skills	Cognitive Development	Affective Development	Logical Thinking	Critical Thinking	Divergent Production	Research Skills	Values Clarification	Group Dynamics	Creativity	Individual Instruction	Group Instruction	Kit	Workbook	Worksheets	Taskcards	Filmstrip(s)	Slides	Audio Tape(s)	Book(s)	Record(s)	Instructional Game	Specialized Equipment	Instructional Guide	Simulation	Other Visual Aids	Duplicating Masters	Transparencies
Interact																														
Puzzle	18.00	I	x	x		x	x		x		x		x					x											x	x	
Search	16.00	I	x	x			x	x	x	x			x					x											x	x	
Science Research Associates, Inc.																														
Researchlab	190.00	I	x	x		x			x				x			x					x		x			x				
Special Learning Corp.																														
Living Things	60.00	I	x	x		x	x	x		x			x	x	x	x			x		x					x	x				x
J. Weston Walsh, Publisher																														
Research Detective	11.00	I	x	x		x	x		x				x													x				x
Xerox Education Publications																														
Tables and Graphs	2.00	I	x	x		x	x						x											x		x				
The Center for the Humanities, Inc.																														
Ecology Sampling Methods and Field Techniques	$170.00	I-S	x	x		x			x				x	x											x		x				
How Do You Figure That? Ways of Problem Solving	170.00	I-S	x	x		x	x		x	x			x	x											x		x				
Special Problems in Library Research	220.00	I-S	x	x		x		x					x	x	x									x		x				
Using Library Resources and Reference Materials	220.00	I-S	x	x		x		x					x	x	x									x		x				
VALUES CLARIFICATION																														
Addison-Wesley Publishing Co.																														
People Projects: Set A	40.00	P	x		x		x		x	x			x	x										x		x				
Coronet																														
Knowing Me, Knowing You	$ 89.00	P	x		x				x	x			x	x					x		x					x				
Eye Gate Media																														
It's Up to You: Vignettes (Self-Discovery)	170.00	P	x	x		x	x		x				x	x	x				x		x					x				

TABLE 2 COMMERCIAL MATERIALS LISTING (continued)

Company and Materials	Cost (Approx.)	Level (Sugg.)	Dimensions of Learning										Format		Components															
			Communication Skills	Cognitive Development	Affective Development	Logical Thinking	Critical Thinking	Divergent Production	Research Skills	Values Clarification	Group Dynamics	Creativity	Individual Instruction	Group Instruction	Kit	Workbook	Worksheets	Taskcards	Filmstrip(s)	Slides	Audio Tape(s)	Book(s)	Record(s)	Instructional Game	Specialized Equipment	Instructional Guide	Simulation	Other Visual Aids	Duplicating Masters	Transparencies
Scholastic, Inc.																														
Becoming Yourself	100.00	P	x	x	x			x		x	x	x		x	x						x	x				x				
Science Research Associates, Inc.																														
Focus on Self-Development: Stage 1, Awareness	290.00	P	x	x	x	x	x	x						x	x	x	x	x	x									x	x	x
Focus on Self-Development: Stage 2, Responding	310.00	P	x	x	x	x	x	x						x	x	x	x	x	x									x	x	x
Addison-Wesley Publishing Co.																														
People Projects: Set B	$ 40.00	P-I	x		x			x		x	x		x	x	x			x								x				
American Guidance Service																														
Toward Affective Development	155.00	P-I	x		x	x	x	x	x	x			x			x	x							x		x		x	x	x
American Institute for Character Education																														
Character Education Curriculum (Grades 1–6; one kit per grade)	70.00	P-I	x	x	x	x	x	x					x															x	x	x
Disseminators of Knowledge, Publishers																														
Effective Communication: A Handbook of Discussion Skills	$ 3.00	P-I	x		x			x	x	x	x		x	x			x									x				
Good Apple, Inc.																														
Connecting Rainbows	8.00	P-I	x		x	x	x	x				x		x			x									x				
B.L. Winch and Associates																														
Feeling Good About Yourself	$109.00	P-I	x		x	x				x				x										x	x					
Getting Along with Others	109.00	P-I	x		x	x				x				x										x	x					
Winston Press, Inc.																														
Deciding for Myself: A Values Clarification Series	11.00	P-I	x		x	x	x			x	x			x		x									x				
Addison-Wesley Publishing Co.																														
People Projects: Set C	40.00	I	x	x				x	x	x	x		x	x	x	x		x								x				

TABLE 2   COMMERCIAL MATERIALS LISTING (continued)

Company and Materials	Cost (Approx.)	Level (Sugg.)	Communication Skills	Cognitive Development	Affective Development	Logical Thinking	Critical Thinking	Divergent Production	Research Skills	Values Clarification	Group Dynamics	Creativity	Individual Instruction	Group Instruction	Kit	Workbook	Worksheets	Taskcards	Filmstrip(s)	Slides	Audio Tape(s)	Book(s)	Record(s)	Instructional Game	Specialized Equipment	Instructional Guide	Simulation	Other Visual Aids	Duplicating Masters	Transparencies
American Guidance Service																														
Transition	168.00	I	x	x		x	x		x	x			x			x	x	x			x					x			x	x
Argus Communications																														
The Best of All Possible Worlds	22.00	I	x	x		x	x		x	x			x			x			x		x	x				x				
Coronet																														
Open-Ended Stories	119.00	I	x	x		x	x		x				x			x			x		x									
Educational Insights, Inc.																														
Decision-making	6.00	I	x	x		x	x		x				x																x	x
Values	6.00	I	x	x		x	x		x				x																x	x
Charles E. Merrill Publishing Co.																														
Decision: A Values Approach to Decision Making	$108.00	I	x	x	x	x	x	x		x	x		x			x	x		x	x		x	x				x			x	
Making Value Judgments: Decisions for Today	7.00	I	x	x	x		x	x		x	x		x			x						x					x				
Milliken Publishing Co.																														
Contemporary Values Series	45.00	I	x	x		x	x		x				x																x	x
Science Research Associates, Inc.																														
Focus on Self-Development Stage Three: Involvement	350.00	I	x	x	x		x	x		x	x		x			x	x		x		x					x		x	x	x	x
Social Studies School Service																														
Innerchange: A Journey into Self-Learning through Group Interaction—Junior High	$175.00	I	x	x	x		x			x	x		x		x	x	x									x			x		
Winston Press, Inc.																														
Values in Action	120.00	I	x	x		x			x	x			x		x	x			x							x		x			
Argus Communications																														
Am I Ok?	34.00	I-S	x	x		x	x		x	x			x			x							x				x			x	x
Feelings and Thoughts	20.00	I-S	x	x		x	x		x	x			x			x			x	x							x				
Friendly and Hostile	20.00	I-S	x	x		x	x		x	x			x			x			x	x							x				
I Am Lovable and Capable	20.00	I-S	x	x		x	x		x	x			x			x			x	x	x						x				

TABLE 2 COMMERCIAL MATERIALS LISTING (continued)

Company and Materials	Cost (Approx.)	Level (Sugg.)	Communication Skills	Cognitive Development	Affective Development	Logical Thinking	Critical Thinking	Divergent Production	Research Skills	Values Clarification	Group Dynamics	Creativity	Individual Instruction	Group Instruction	Kit	Workbook	Worksheets	Taskcards	Filmstrip(s)	Slides	Audio Tape(s)	Book(s)	Record(s)	Instructional Game	Specialized Equipment	Instructional Guide	Simulation	Other Visual Aids	Duplicating Masters	Transparencies
If I'm in Charge Here, Why Is Everybody Laughing?	$ 35.00	I-S	x	x		x	x			x	x		x	x					x		x	x				x			x	
If You Don't Know Where You're Going, You'll Probably End Up Somewhere Else	35.00	I-S	x	x		x	x			x	x		x	x					x		x	x				x				x
Lifeline	50.00	I-S	x	x		x	x			x	x		x	x		x	x				x					x				
Let's Get Organized	20.00	I-S	x	x		x	x			x	x		x	x					x			x				x				
Making Sense of Our Lives	39.00	I-S	x	x		x	x			x	x		x	x	x											x		x		
Meeting Yourself Halfway	19.00	I-S	x	x		x	x			x	x		x	x								x								x
Roles and Goals	20.00	I-S	x	x		x	x			x	x		x	x					x			x				x				
Strike It Rich	$ 20.00	I-S	x	x		x	x			x	x		x	x					x			x				x				
Take the Road to Creativity and Get Off Your Dead End	35.00	I-S	x	x		x	x			x	x		x	x					x		x	x				x				x
Taking Charge of Your Life	13.00	I-S	x	x		x	x			x	x		x	x							x					x				x
Truth and Consequences	20.00	I-S	x		x	x	x			x	x		x	x					x			x				x				
Vulture	22.00	I-S	x		x	x	x			x	x		x	x					x			x				x				
Why Am I Afraid to Tell You Who I Am?	40.00	I-S	x		x	x	x			x	x		x	x					x		x	x				x		x		
Winners and Losers	23.00	I-S	x		x	x	x			x	x		x	x					x		x	x				x				
You Have to Want Something	20.00	I-S	x		x	x	x			x	x		x	x					x			x				x				
Creative Learning Systems, Inc.																														
Dilemma	$ 36.00	I-S	x	x	x					x	x		x	x										x	x	x	x			
Lifestyle Auction	20.00	I-S	x	x	x					x	x		x	x										x		x	x			
Self-Awareness Auction	20.00	I-S	x	x	x					x	x		x	x										x		x	x			
Friendship Press																														
Values: A Friendship Orbis Game	6.00	I-S	x	x						x			x											x		x	x			
Globe Book Co., Inc.																														
A Matter for Judgment: Stories of Moral Conflict	4.00	I-S	x	x		x	x			x			x									x				x				
Interact																														
Death	7.00	I-S	x	x	x	x	x	x	x				x	x	x	x										x				

TABLE 2 COMMERCIAL MATERIALS LISTING (continued)

Company and Materials	Cost (Approx.)	Level (Sugg.)	Communication Skills	Cognitive Development	Affective Development	Logical Thinking	Critical Thinking	Divergent Production	Research Skills	Values Clarification	Group Dynamics	Creativity	Individual Instruction	Group Instruction	Kit	Workbook	Worksheets	Taskcards	Filmstrip(s)	Slides	Audio Tape(s)	Book(s)	Record(s)	Instructional Game	Specialized Equipment	Instructional Guide	Simulation	Other Visual Aids	Duplicating Masters	Transparencies
			Dimensions of Learning										Format		Components															
The Center for the Humanities, Inc.																														
Clarifying Your Values: Guidelines for Living	$170.00	S	x		x	x	x			x	x		x	x					x							x				
Deciding Right from Wrong: The Dilemma of Morality Today	170.00	S	x		x	x	x			x	x		x	x					x							x				
Freedom and Responsibility: A Question of Values	170.00	S	x		x	x	x			x	x		x	x					x							x				
Human Values in an Age of Technology	170.00	S	x		x	x	x			x	x		x	x					x							x				
Man's Search for Identity	170.00	S	x		x	x	x			x	x		x	x					x							x				
Perspectives on Death	170.00	S	x		x	x	x			x	x		x	x					x							x				
Who Am I? Where Did I Come From? Where Am I Going? The Eternal Questions	$170.00	S	x		x	x	x			x	x		x	x					x							x				
Eye Gate Media																														
Understanding Values	102.00	S	x		x	x	x			x			x	x	x				x				x			x				
Values for Living	102.00	S	x		x	x	x			x			x	x	x				x				x			x				
Greenhaven Press																														
Isms Series of Opposing Viewpoints	36.00	S	x	x	x	x	x	x		x	x		x	x										x		x				
Opposing Viewpoints Pamphlets Series	178.00	S	x	x	x	x	x	x		x	x		x	x											x	x				
Opposing Viewpoints Series	$120.00	S	x	x	x	x	x	x		x	x		x	x											x	x				
Photo Study Cards	15.00	S	x		x	x	x			x	x		x	x														x	x	
Guidance Associates, Inc.																														
Clarifying Your Values: Guidelines for Living	150.00	S	x		x		x			x	x		x	x					x				x			x				
Values in a Democracy: Making Ethical Decisions	220.00	S	x	x	x	x	x			x	x		x	x					x				x			x				x
Interact																														
Five Faces	7.00	S	x	x	x	x	x	x	x	x	x		x	x	x	x	x									x				
Love	$ 7.00	S	x	x	x	x	x	x	x	x	x		x	x	x	x	x									x				

TABLE 2   COMMERCIAL MATERIALS LISTING (continued)

Company and Materials	Cost (Approx.)	Level (Sugg.)	Communication Skills	Cognitive Development	Affective Development	Logical Thinking	Critical Thinking	Divergent Production	Research Skills	Values Clarification	Group Dynamics	Creativity	Individual Instruction	Group Instruction	Kit	Workbook	Worksheets	Taskcards	Filmstrip(s)	Slides	Audio Tape(s)	Book(s)	Record(s)	Instructional Game	Specialized Equipment	Instructional Guide	Simulation	Other Visual Aids	Duplicating Masters	Transparencies
Prentice-Hall Media																														
Exploring Moral Values	120.00	S	x	x	x	x				x	x		x						x	x							x			
Simile II																														
Where Do You Draw the Line?	25.00	S	x			x	x	x		x	x		x											x	x	x				
Social Studies School Service																														
Innerchange: A Journey into Self-Learning through Group Interaction—Senior High	175.00	S	x	x	x	x				x	x		x	x	x									x		x				
Value Questionnaires for United States History	5.00	S	x	x	x	x	x			x	x		x															x		x

PUBLISHERS/DISTRIBUTORS AND ADDRESSES

Academic Therapy Publications
20 Commercial Boulevard
Novato, CA 94947

Activity Resources Co., Inc.
P.O. Box 4875
Hayward, CA 94540

Addison-Wesley Publishing Co., Inc.
Reading, MA 01867

American Guidance Service
Publishers' Building
Circle Pines, MN 55014

American Institute for Character Education
P.O. Box 12617
San Antonio, TX 78212

Ampersand Press
691 26th Street
Oakland, CA 94612

Ann Arbor Publishers, Inc.
P.O. Box 7249
Naples, FL 33941

Argus Communications
One DLM Park
P.O. Box 6000
Allen, TX 75002

Benefic Press
1250 6th Avenue
San Diego, CA 92101

**California Learning
   Simulations**
750 Lurline Drive
Foster City, CA 94404

Carolina Biological Supply Co.
Burlington, NC 27215

**The Center for the Humanities,
   Inc.**
Communications Park
P.O. Box 1000
Mount Kisco, NY 10549

Central Scientific Co., Inc.
11222 Melrose Avenue
Franklin Park, IL 60131

Charlotte's Web
P.O. Box 1786
Sausalito, CA 94966

Coronet
65 East South Water Street
Chicago, IL 60601

Creative Learning Press
P.O. Box 320
Mansfield Center, CT 06250

Creative Learning Systems, Inc.
936 C Street
San Diego, CA 92101

Creative Publications
P.O.Box 10328
Palo Alto, CA 94303

Creative Teaching Associates
P.O. Box 7766
Fresno, CA 93727

Creative Teaching Press, Inc.
P.O. Box P–92
Huntington Beach, CA 92647

Cuisenaire Co. of America, Inc.
12 Church Street
New Rochelle, NY 10805

Curriculum Associates, Inc.
5 Esquire Road
North Billerica, MA 01862

**Disseminators of Knowledge,
   Publishers**
71 Radcliffe Road
Buffalo, NY 14214

Edmund Scientific Co.
101 East Gloucester Pike
Barrington, NJ 08007

Educational Activities, Inc.
Box 392
Freeport, NY 11520

**Educational Development
   Corporation**
8141 E. 44th Street
Tulsa, OK 74145

Educational Insights, Inc.
150 West Carob Street
Compton, CA 90220

Educulture
Suite 150
1 Dubuque Plaza
Dubuque, IA 52001

EMC Publishing
300 York Avenue
St. Paul, MN 55101

EMI
P.O. Box 4272
Madison, WI 53711

Encyclopedia Britannica
  Educational Corp.
425 North Michigan Avenue
Chicago, IL 60611

Eye Gate Media
P.O. Box 303
Jamaica, NY 11435

Fawcett Book Group
1515 Broadway
New York, NY 10036

Fisher Scientific Co.
Educational Materials Division
4901 West Le Moyne
Chicago, IL 60650

Foxtail Press
P.O. Box 2996
La Habra, CA 90631

Friendship Press
P.O. Box 37844
Cincinnati, OH 45237

Geo Books
Room 401
171 2nd Street
San Francisco, CA 94105

Globe Book Co., Inc.
50 West 23rd Street
New York, NY 10010

Good Apple, Inc.
P.O. Box 299
Carthage, IL 62321

Goodyear Books
1900 East Lake Avenue
Glenview, IL 60025

Greenhaven Press, Inc.
577 Shoreview Park Road
St. Paul, MN 55112

Guidance Associates, Inc.
Communications Park
P.O. Box 3000
Mt. Kisco, NY 10549

Harcourt Brace and Jovanovich,
  Inc.
757 3rd Avenue
New York, NY 10017

Harper & Row Publishers, Inc.
10 East 53rd Street
New York, NY 10022

Hayes School Publishing Co.,
  Inc.
321 Pennwood Avenue
Wilkinsburg, PA 15221

D.C. Heath and Co.
125 Spring Street
Lexington, MA 02173

Humanics Limited
P.O. Box 7447
Atlanta, GA 30309

Ideal School Supply Co.
11000 South Lavergne Avenue
Oak Lawn, IL 60453

Innovative Sciences, Inc.
Park Square Station
P.O. Box 15129
Stamford, CT 06901

**Institute for the Advancement
of Philosophy for Children**
Montclair State College
Upper Montclair, NJ 07043

Interact
P.O. Box 997G
Lakeside, CA 92040

Learning Seed Co.
21250 Andover
Kildeer, IL 60047

The Learning Works
P.O. Box 6187
Santa Barbara, CA 93111

Listos Publications
P.O. Box 666
Coeur d'Alene, ID 83814

Little, Brown and Co.
34 Beacon Street
Boston, MA 02106

**Charles E. Merrill Publishing
Co.**
1300 Alum Creek Drive
Columbus, OH 43216

Midwest Publications
P.O. Box 448
Pacific Grove, CA 93950

Milliken Publishing Co.
1100 Research Boulevard
St. Louis, MO 63132

Penichet Publishing Co.
1607 Hope Street
P.O. Box 669
South Pasadena, CA 91030

Pennant Educational Materials
8265 Commercial Street
Suite 14
La Mesa, CA 92041

Pitman Learning, Inc.
6 Davis Drive
Belmont, CA 94002

Prentice-Hall Media
150 White Plains Road
Tarrytown, NY 10591

**Frank Schaeffer Publications,
Inc.**
1028 Via Mirabel
Dept. 34
Palos Verdes Estates, CA 90274

Scholastic, Inc.
904 Sylvan Avenue
Englewood Cliffs, NJ 07632

Schoolmasters Science
745 State Circle
P.O. Box 1941
Ann Arbor, MI 48104

**Science Research Associates,
Inc.**
155 North Wacker Drive
Chicago, IL 60606

Dale Seymour Publications
P.O. Box 10888
Palo Alto, CA 94303

Simile II
P.O. Box 910
Del Mar, CA 92014

Social Studies School Service
10000 Culver Boulevard
P.O. Box 802, Dept. 12
Culver City, CA 90230

Society for Visual Education, Inc.
1345 Diversey Parkway
Chicago, IL 60614

Special Learning Corp.
42 Boston Post Road
Guilford, CT 06437

Stallard Press
Claremont Educational
  Resources
P.O. Box 1116
Ontario, CA 91762

Structure of the Intellect Institute
343 Richmond Street
El Segundo, CA 90245

Sunburst Communications
39 Washington Avenue
Room 5252
Pleasantville, NY 10570

Synergetics
P.O. Box 84
East Windsor Hill, CT 06028

Teaching Resources Corp.
50 Pond Park Road
Hingham, MA 02043

Trillium Press
Madison Square Station
P.O. Box 921
New York, NY 10159

Troll Associates
320 Rt. 17
Mahwah, NJ 07430

J. Weston Walsh, Publisher
P.O. Box 658
Portland, ME 04104

WFF'N Proof Learning Games Associates
1490 South Boulevard
Ann Arbor, MI 48104

B.L. Winch and Associates
45 Hitching Post Drive
Building 23 NS
Rolling Hills Estates, CA 90274

Winston Press, Inc.
430 Oak Grove
Minneapolis, MN 55403

Xerox Education Publications
1250 Fairwood Avenue
Columbus, OH 43216

DISTRIBUTORS SPECIALIZING IN MATERIALS FOR THE GIFTED

Dandy Lion Publications
P.O. Box 190, Dept. AD
San Luis Obispo, CA
  93406–0190

Engine-Uity, Ltd.
P.O. Box 9610
Phoenix, AZ 85608

G/C/T Catalog
P.O. Box 66707
Mobile, AL 36660

Opportunities for Learning, Inc.
8950 Lurline Avenue, Dept.
  FR 28
Chatsworth, CA 91311

A.W. Peller and Associates, Inc.
124 Rhea Avenue
Hawthorne, NJ 07506

Resources for the Gifted, Inc.
3421 North 44th Street
Phoenix, AZ 85018

Thinking Works
P.O. Box 468
St. Augustine, FL 32084–0468

The Wright Group
7620 Miramar Road, Suite 4100
San Diego, CA 92126

Zephyr
430 South Essex Lane
Tucson, AZ 85711

4 Selected Professional References

Those teachers, administrators, counselors, curriculum specialists, directors of gifted education programs, and other interested professionals, and parents who are concerned with theory as well as teaching techniques and practical suggestions for the education of gifted students, make up the audience for whom this chapter is intended. An objective, annotated bibliography of selected references pertinent to the education of gifted students at the elementary and secondary school levels is offered according to the following topical areas: gifted education; arts, humanities, and music; computers; creativity; critical thinking, logic, and problem solving; futurism; group dynamics; leadership; math and science; reading and language arts; social studies; values clarification; and related topics.

Within these areas, sources of information on the following concepts and issues may be located: identification, program formulation, curriculum development, and specific teaching strategies which include cognitive and affective development and the stimulation of creative processes. Additional information may be found on teacher education, culturally diverse gifted, and gifted/handicapped.

Books and textbooks, both hard- and soft-cover, are included, while smaller publications, such as leaflets, pamphlets, and monographs are excluded. Because there are so many publications that are either primarily developed at the local and state levels or privately published, such resources are not included within this section. These sources of additonal information on the gifted and talented can easily be obtained from state and local directors of programs for the gifted.

Each reference is followed by a brief objective annotation describing the salient features of the book. A list of the publishers of these resource and reference books and their addresses is included at the end of this chapter.

GIFTED EDUCATION

Abraham, Willard. *Common sense about gifted children.* New York: Harper & Row, 1958.

The author provides specific suggestions for all factors involved in the socioeducational process for gifted students: the parent, educational personnel, and the community.

Abraham, Willard, et al. *Gifts, talents, and the very young: Early childhood education for gifted/talented.* Ventura, Calif.: National/State Leadership Training Institute, Office of the Ventura County Superintendent of Schools, 1977.

This is a compilation of presentations from the Institute on Gifted/Talented Early Childhood Education in January, 1977, in Oxnard, California. Topics include nature and characteristics of young gifted children and suggestions for programming.

Alexander, P., and Muia, J. *Gifted education: A comprehensive roadmap.* Rockville, Md.: Aspen Systems Corp., 1981.

Various topics are addressed, including identification, needs assessment, establishing and determining program format, curriculum, financing, and evaluating programs. Charts, forms, checklists, and diagrams are given.

Anthony, J.B., and Anthony, M.M. *The gifted and talented: A bibliography and resource guide.* Pittsfield, Mass.: Berkshire Community Press, 1981.

This reference book contains more than 3,200 citations. The bibliography includes: identification, characteristics, education, considerations, special issues, and relevant research. Diagnostic instruments, media aids, organizations and state consultants, and publications and publishers are among the resources listed.

Arnold, A., et al. *Secondary programs for the gifted/talented.* Ventura, Calif.: National/State Leadership Training Institute, Office of the Ventura County Superintendent of Schools, 1981.

Programs described include independent study, creativity in science, fine and performing arts, and humanities. Administering programs at the secondary level is discussed.

Aschner, M., and Bish, C. (Eds.) *Productive thinking in education.* Washington D.C.: National Education Association, 1965.

Leading educators offer viewpoints on intelligence, and the influence of motivation and personality on productive thinking. Assessment of productive thinking and the role of education in fostering it are explored.

Ashley, Rosalind M. *Activities for motivating and teaching bright children.* Englewood Cliff, N.J.: Parker Publishing, 1973.

Suggestions directed at the regular classroom teacher to promote individualization in the areas of social studies, art, science, and math for gifted students are presented. A section on games for challenging bright students is included.

Bagley, M., and Lynch, V.L. *Units: A resource guide of differentiated learning experiences for gifted elementary students.* Woodcliff Lake, N.J.: New Dimensions for the 80's Publishers, 1981.

For each unit, there are learner objectives, major concepts, general content areas, activities, and resources and references. Units cover topics in language arts, science, and social studies.

Baldwin, A., Gear, G., and Lucito, L. *Educational planning for the gifted: Overcoming cultural, geographic, and socioeconomic impediments.* Reston, Va.: Council for Exceptional Children, 1978.

Identification, programming, and school-community relationships are discussed in relation to culturally diverse gifted students. Practical suggestions are offered for teachers, administrators, and psychologists.

Barbe, W.B. *Psychology and education of the gifted: Selected readings.* New York: John Wiley and Sons, 1965.

A compilation of articles by leaders in the education of the gifted which include historical aspects of the movement for the education of the gifted, as well as current trends in the fields provided. Topics include identification, characteristics, creativity, socio-emotional correlates, hereditary aspects, and educational planning.

Barbe, W.B., and Renzulli, J.S. *Psychology and education of the gifted,* 2nd ed. New York: Halsted Press, 1975.

This is a revision of Barbe's earlier work.

Barbe, W.J., and Renzulli, J.S. (Eds.) *Psychology and education of the gifted,* 3rd ed. New York: Irvington Publishers, 1981.

This is a revision of Barbe and Renzulli's earlier work. Additional articles focus on new issues in the education of the gifted and talented.

Barton, P., et al. *A new generation of leadership: Education for the gifted in leadership.* Ventura, Calif.: National/State Leadership Training Institute, Office of the Ventura County Superintendent of Schools, 1976.

A practical guide for the identification of leadership potential and an overview of programs for developing leadership skills are the major thrusts of this publication.

Baskin, B.H., and Harris, K.H. *Books for the gifted.* New York: R.R. Bowker, 1980.

Described in this book are the identification of gifted children and their characteristics. In addition, a listing and description of intellectually challenging books is given.

Birnbaum, M., et al. *Ideas for urban/rural gifted/talented: Case histories and program plans.* Ventura, Calif.: National/State Leadership Training Institute, Office of the Ventura County Superintendent of Schools, 1977.

Problems in providing rural programs for gifted and talented students are discussed. Examples of existing programs are provided. An urban independent study program for gifted and talented high school students is described.

Birnbaum, M., Blanning, J., Caudill, G., and Plowman, P. *Ideas for urban/rural gifted/talented.* Ventura, Calif.: National/State Leadership Training Institute, Office of the Ventura County Superintendent of Schools, 1979.

Ideas for program development and advocacy are discussed in this publication.

Bostick, L., et al. *Educating the preschool/primary gifted and talented.* Ventura, Calif.: National/State Leadership Training Institute, Office of the Ventura County Superintendent of Schools, 1980.

Ideas on identification, curriculum and programming, and working with parents are offered. Six programs are detailed.

Boston, B. *The sorcerer's apprentice: A case study in the role of the mentor.* Reston, Va.: Council for Exceptional Children, 1976.

Based on Carlos Castaneda's tetralogy of books, the relationship between mentor and pupil is examined. Implications for the education of the gifted are extracted.

Boston, B. (Ed.) *Gifted and talented: Developing elementary and secondary school programs.* Reston, Va.: Council for Exceptional Children, 1975.

Experts in the field of gifted education comment on the initiation of a gifted program, instructional planning, disadvantaged gifted, and the importance of educating the gifted. An interview with Dr. James J. Gallagher reveals his current thinking on gifted education.

Boston, B. (Ed.) *Resource manual of information on gifted education.* Reston, Va.: Council for Exceptional Children, 1975.

This reference includes state, regional, and federal agencies involved in the education of the gifted and talented. A listing of films and a bibliography are included.

Brandwein, P. *The gifted student as future scientist.* Ventura, Calif.: National/State Leadership Training Institute, Office of the Ventura County Superintendent of Schools, 1981.

A reprint of a previous work in which the author discusses self-identification and other methods to determine those outstanding in science. Characteristics of these students and who should teach them are considered.

Bridges, S. *Problems of the gifted child: I.Q. 150.* New York: Crane, Russak, 1974.

The main focus of this book is upon the characteristics, needs, and problems of highly gifted children. Diverse forms of giftedness are discussed. Special attention is devoted to the problems confronted by gifted children.

Buehler, C. (Ed.) *Directory of learning resources for the gifted and talented.* Waterford, Conn.: Croft-NEI Publications, 1981.

A compendium of information, including current trends and issues, periodicals, and professional training centers. State agencies, organizations and associations, as well as national organizations and associations, are presented.

Burks, B., Jensen, D., and Terman, L. *Genetic studies of genius. Volume III, The promise of youth: Follow-up studies of a thousand gifted children.* Stanford, Calif.: Stanford University Press, 1930.

The first follow-up study on the gifted subjects in the Terman study included a verification of data previously collected. An in-depth analysis of family statistics and sibling tests is an integral component.

Burt, Cyril. *The gifted child.* New York: Halsted Press, 1976.

An account of the nature of intelligence, the inheritability of intelligence, and the relationship to giftedness is presented. Early recognition, needs and problems, and specialized educational programming for the gifted are described.

Butterfield, S.H., et al. *Developing IEPs for the gifted/talented.* Ventura, Calif.: National/State Leadership Training Institute, Office of the Ventura County Superintendent of Schools, 1979.

Contained in this book of readings are articles on the development of Individual Education Plan for gifted, talented, and creative students. A potential model for diagnosing and matching curriculum to cognitive patterns is discussed. Many examples with forms are given.

Ciabotti, P., and Crocker, H. *Career awareness day.* Mansfield Center, Conn.: Creative Learning Press, 1981.

Forms, letters, and student activities for conducting a career awareness day are presented.

Clark, B. *Growing up gifted,* 2nd ed. Columbus, Ohio: Charles E. Merrill Publishing, 1983.

This book focuses on the gifted student at home and at school. One chapter explores areas of the future: brain research, biofeedback, parapsychology, and transpersonal education. Listings of tests and forms for case studies are provided.

Clendening, C., and Davies, R. *Creating programs for the gifted.* New York: R.R. Bowker, 1980.

Guidelines for establishing programs for the gifted are given, and sixty field-tested educational programs are detailed. Advanced Placement course descriptions are outlined.

Clendenning, C., and Davies, R. *Challenging the gifted: Curriculum enrichment and acceleration models.* New York: R.R. Bowker, 1983.

Teaching/learning projects emphasizing enrichment, acceleration, individualization, and seminars, which have all been field-tested, are given. A variety of media and technological references are provided.

Cline, S. *A practical guide to independent study: Instructional manuals for students and teachers.* (Rev. ed.) New York: Trillium Press, 1982.

Establishing and implementing an independent study program for gifted students is detailed. Appropriate topics and various forms are provided.

Coffee, K., et al. *Parentspeak on gifted and talented children.* Ventura, Calif.: National/State Leadership Training Institute, Office of the Ventura County Superintendent of Schools, 1976.

Topics included in this publication are reasons for specialized education of gifted and talented, program promotion, and practical suggestions for organizing state and local groups.

Correll, M. *Teaching the gifted and talented.* Bloomington, Ind.: Phi Delta Kappa, 1978.

The definition, characteristics, and approaches to educating the gifted and talented are discussed. The roles of parents and community leaders are also set forth.

Cox, C., et al. *Genetic studies of genius. Volume II, The early mental traits of three hundred geniuses.* Stanford, Calif.: Stanford University Press, 1926.

Biographical accounts of the lives and works of 300 persons of eminence in various fields are presented. Estimated intelligence quotients were calculated based on accomplishments.

Croley, J., and Bagley, M. *Suppose the wolf were an octopus.* Woodcliff Lake, N.J.: New Dimensions for the 80's Publishers, 1981.

Levels of questioning based on Bloom's Taxonomy are given for a wide range of books for the primary grades. Included are professional references and selected examples of children's literature.

Crosby, N., and Marten, E. *Don't teach! Let me learn!* Buffalo, N.Y.: Disseminators of Knowledge Publishers, 1981.

A series of six books with a manual is designed to develop creativity and independent study skills. Topics include science, humanities, social science, and communications.

Crow, Lester, and Crow, Alice (Eds.) *Educating the academically able.* New York: David McKay, 1963.

This book directs itself to basic principles and practices dealing with the education of the gifted. Curricula and specific programs for gifted learners are described.

Cutts, N., and Moseley, N. *Teaching the bright and gifted.* Englewood Cliffs, N.J.: Prentice-Hall, 1957.

Identification, needs, programming, and guidance for the gifted are topics discussed. Also included is a discussion of the underachieving gifted student.

Daniels, P. *Teaching the gifted/learning disabled child.* Rockville, Maryland: Aspen Systems Corporation, 1983.

Topics discussed are characteristics and traits, early identification, and diagnostic aspects. Specific abilities units are given for word recognition, classification skills, levels of abstraction, appreciating relevancy, oral language facility, and vocabulary development.

DeHann, R., and Havighurst, R. *Educating gifted children.* Chicago: University of Chicago Press, 1961.

Based on experiences in the Quincy Youth Development Project, the authors discuss administration of gifted programs, motivation, developing creativity, community resources, and teaching the gifted in the regular classroom.

Delp, J., and Martinson, R. *The gifted and talented: A handbook for parents.* Ventura, Calif.: National/State Leadership Training Institute, Office of the Ventura County Superintendent of Schools, 1975.

A guide for forming parent organizations is presented in this book. The identification process and the needs of gifted students are treated. Practical suggestions for parents are enumerated.

Dennis, W., and Dennis, M. (Eds.) *The intellectually gifted: An overview*. New York: Grune and Stratton, 1976.

The editors have compiled twenty-five articles concerned with the gifted. Articles by Terman, Hollingworth, Gallagher, Weiner, Binet, Cox, Stanley, and Havighurst are among those presented. Topics include characteristics, case studies, personality factors, creativity, and educational programming.

Dickinson, R. *Caring for the gifted*. West Hanover, Mass.: Christopher Publishing House, 1970.

Ideas for parents and teachers of the gifted are contained in this book. Practical educational suggestions are provided.

Durr, W. *The gifted student*. New York: Oxford University Press, 1964.

The emphasis in this book is on educational methodologies and programs designed to allow gifted students to maximize their potential.

Ehrlich, V. *Gifted children*. Englewood Cliffs, N.J.: Prentice-Hall, 1982.

In this guide for parents and teachers, the topics of definition, characteristics, and appropriate programming are discussed. In addition, information on career education and the law and the gifted are presented.

Emmerly, T., Frey, C., and Gilmar, S. *A gifted program that works*. Johnstown, Pa.: Mafex Associates, 1982.

Suggestions for a successful program are offered. Also included are ideas for creative and journalistic writing, architectural design, debating, and the photographic essay.

Epstein, C.B. *The gifted and talented: Programs that work*. Arlington, Va.: National School of Public Relations Association, 1979.

This book contains descriptions of the current status of gifted education in many states. Additionally, selected programs for the gifted and talented are described.

Feldhusen, J.F., and Treffinger, D.G. *Creative thinking and problem solving in gifted education.* Dubuque, Iowa: Kendall/Hunt Publishing, 1980.

The book focuses on the teaching of creative thinking and problem-solving skills for the gifted, including those from economically disadvantaged homes. Descriptions of materials and books are provided.

Fitzgerald, E., et al. (Eds.) *The first national conference on disadvantaged gifted.* Ventura, Calif.: National/State Leadership Training Institute, Office of the Ventura County Superintendent of Schools, 1975.

A compilation of papers dealing with the identification of culturally different gifted, program development, and evaluation of programs is provided.

Fleigler, L. *Curriculum planning for the gifted.* Englewood Cliffs, N.J.: Prentice-Hall, 1961.

Development and implementation of specialized curricula for gifted students are delineated. Administrative and teaching responsibilities are included.

Flowers, J., Horsman, J., and Schwartz, B. *Raising your gifted child.* Englewood Cliffs, N.J.: Prentice-Hall, 1982.

Parental concerns for their gifted children are addressed in this book. Creativity, the underachieving gifted child, and the influences of the advanced child on the family structure are discussed.

Fortna, R., and Boston, B. *Testing the gifted child: An interpretation in lay language.* Reston, Va.: Council for Exceptional Children, 1976.

A brief overview is given of a few tests used in screening and identification of the gifted and talented.

Fox, L., Brody, L., and Tobin, L. *Learning disabled gifted children: Identification and programming.* Baltimore: University Park Press, 1983.

The results of a three-year research study on gifted children with learning disabilities are presented. Emphasis is given to appropriate identification measures and educational programming.

Fox, L., and Durden, W. Educating verbally gifted youth. Bloomington, Ind.: Phi Delta Kappa, 1982.

Described in this book are the identification and a model program for verbally gifted youth. Also discussed are the implementation of programs and the selection of teachers.

Frasier, M., and Carland, J. *Dictionary of gifted, talented, and creative education term.* New York: Trillium Press, 1982.

In addition to the definitions of terms, this book contains a bibliography, list of associations, journals and publications, and tests.

Frederickson, R., and Rothney, J. *Recognizing and assisting multipotential youth.* Columbus, Ohio: Charles E. Merrill Publishing, 1972.

This collection of readings centers on the identification, development, and provisions for multipotential youth. These individuals are defined as those who can develop any number of competencies to a high level while showing a high degree of adaptability. Topics included are the relationship between creativity and intelligence, national and state organizations and programs, counseling needs and special problems of females and culturally different gifted students.

Freehill, M. *Gifted children: Their psychology and education.* New York: Macmillan, 1961.

A variety of topics pertinent to the education of gifted children are treated. Included are sections on characteristics, intellectual development, observational and psychological techniques of identification, stereotypes, sex differences, learning needs, program arrangements, and the talented/gifted distinction. Chapters on adapting various subjects in the curriculum (mathematics, language arts, science, and social studies) for the gifted are also encompassed in this book.

Freehill, M. *Gifted children: Their psychology and education.* Ventura, Calif.: National/State Leadership Training Institute, Office of the Ventura County Superintendent of Schools, 1982.

A reprint of an earlier work by the same author includes information on identification by observation and by test and curriculum suggestions in foreign language, aesthetics, mathematics, language arts, social studies, and science.

Freeman, D., and Stuart, V. *Resources for gifted children in the New York area.* New York: Trillium Press, 1979.

This resource guide contains information on schools and school programs for the gifted. In addition, selected activities for the gifted in the New York area are listed.

Freeman, J. *Gifted children.* Baltimore, Md.: University Park Press, 1979.

Described is the first investigation of the gifted child in his or her own environment. The results of the Gulbenkian Project, which compared labeled and nonlabeled gifted with normal students, are given and discussed.

French, J. (Ed.) *Educating the gifted: A book of readings.* New York: Holt, Rinehart and Winston, 1964.

This survey of literature in gifted education includes such topics as identification, administrative programming arrangements, guidance, creativity, and underachievement.

Friedman, P. *Teaching the gifted and talented in oral communication and leadership.* Washington, D.C.: National Education Association, 1980.

Described are characteristics and means of identifying students gifted in speech communication and leadership. Strategies for teaching the gifted in oral communication skills are given.

Gallagher, James J. *Research summary on gifted child education.* Springfield, Ill.: Office of the Superintendent of Public Instruction, 1966.

A summary of research and studies on the gifted prior to 1966, this focuses on identification, programming, the culturally different, underachievers, and needed personnel.

Gallagher, James J. *Teaching the gifted child,* 2nd ed. Newton, Mass.: Allyn and Bacon, 1975.

Characteristics, identification, program planning, and modification of the subject matter areas of language arts, science, mathematics, and social studies are explored. Productive thinking, creativity, and the nature and needs of the culturally different gifted and underachieving gifted are also incorporated.

Gallagher, James J. (Ed.) *Gifted children: Reaching their potential.* Jerusalem: Kollek and Son, 1979.

Twenty-six articles are contained in this volume on the proceedings of the Second World Conference on Gifted Children held in San Francisco in 1977. The papers deal with program suggestions and design, research, and a variety of issues related to giftedness.

Gallagher, James J., Gowan, J.C., Passow, A.H., and Torrance, E.P. *Issues in gifted education.* Ventura, Calif.: National/State Leadership Training Institute, Office of the Ventura County Superintendent of Schools, 1979.

Issues discussed in this volume are: creativity and identification; the use of developmental stage theory and creativity; and research needed in gifted education. Secondary program alternatives and examples are given.

Gallagher, James J., and Kinney, L. (Eds.) *Talent delayed—talent denied: A conference report.* Reston, Va.: Foundation for Exceptional Children, 1974.

Various experts in the field of culturally different gifted students explore possible solutions to identification, program planning, and subsequent benefit to society.

George, W., and Bartkovich, K. *Teaching the gifted and talented in the mathematics classroom.* Washington, D.C.: National Education Association, 1980.

Identification, teaching strategies, and evaluation of mathematics for the gifted are discussed. Suggestions for teacher and textbook selection are given.

George, W.C., Cohn, S.J., and Stanley, J.C. *Educating the gifted: Acceleration and enrichment.* Baltimore, Md.: Johns Hopkins University Press, 1979.

The book is a compendium of the proceedings of the Ninth Annual Hyman Blumberg Symposium on Research in Early Childhood Education. Key features of acceleration and enrichment are discussed by leaders in the education of the gifted and talented.

Ginsberg, G., and Harrison, C. *How to help your gifted child: A handbook for parents and teachers.* New York: Monarch Press, 1977.

Historical development and current activities of The Gifted Child Society are presented. Practical strategies for implementing out-of-school programs are suggested.

Goertzel, V., and Goertzel, M. *Cradles of eminence.* Boston: Little, Brown, 1978.

This is a study of the childhoods, parentage, educational provisions, and attitudes of 400 eminent men and women of our century.

Goertzel, M.G., Goertzel, V., and Goertzel, T.G. *Three hundred eminent personalities.* San Francisco: Jossey-Bass, Publishers, 1978.

Failure-prone and famous fathers; birth order; mental, physical, and behavioral problems; and marriage and sexuality are discussed for 316 eminent personalities. Political, literary, artistic, and other personalities are detailed.

Gold, M. *Education of the intellectually gifted.* Columbus, Ohio: Charles E. Merrill Publishing, 1965.

Gifted students and appropriate educational procedures for them are discussed in this book which includes sections on characteristics, identification, creativity, program planning, guidance, and teaching methodologies for the various content areas.

Gold, M. *Education of the gifted/talented.* Ventura, Calif.: National/ State Leadership Training Institute, Office of the Superintendent of Schools, 1982.

In this reprint of his book, Gold updates his previous work from 1965 to 1982. The original work addressed such topics as motivation and underachievement, guidance, thinking, and teachers of the gifted.

Gowan, J. *Annotated bibliography on the academically talented.* Washington, D.C.: National Education Association, 1961.

An annotated bibliography covering the major journal articles and books on the gifted and talented prior to 1961.

Gowan, J., and Bruch, C. *The academically talented student and guidance.* Boston: Houghton Mifflin, 1970.

The major focus is upon the counseling and guidance needs of gifted students. Included are portions on atypical gifted students such as the culturally different, females, and the highly gifted. Suggestions are provided to teachers and counselors.

Gowan, J., and Demos, G. *Education and guidance of the ablest.* Springfield, Ill.: Charles C. Thomas, Publisher, 1964.

Programming for the gifted is described in detail. Concepts of superior intelligence and appropriate educational modifications are also included.

Gowan, J., Khatena, J., and Torrance, E. (Eds.) *Educating the ablest: A book of readings.* Itasca, Ill.: F.E. Peacock, Publishers, 1979.

This book of readings focuses on the history of gifted education, curriculum, guidance, characteristics, women, identification, and teachers and teacher training. In addition, there are several chapters on creativity and the creative process.

Gowan, J., and Torrance, E.P. (Eds.) *Educating the ablest.* Itasca, Ill.: F.E. Peacock, Publishers, 1971.

A book of readings focusing on the identification of the gifted, models for encouraging creative teaching, the role of the counselor, the gifted dropout, and the disadvantaged gifted child is presented.

Gray, W. *Challenging the gifted and talented through mentor-assisted enrichment projects.* Bloomington, Indiana: Phi Delta Kappa, 1983.

Steps for establishing a mentor-assisted program are discussed: proposing an enrichment project, determining a final project plan, carrying out the project, and completing and presenting the project. Descriptions of twelve projects are provided.

Grossi, J.A. *Model state policy, legislation and state plan toward the education of gifted and talented students.* Reston, Va.: Council for Exceptional Children, 1980.

A model state policy for the gifted and talented and a model statute to promote the education of gifted and talented students are given. Considerations in the development of a state plan, including identification, procedural safeguards, service delivery, personnel development, and fiscal management are discussed.

Grost, A. *Genius in residence.* Englewood Cliffs, N.J.: Prentice-Hall, 1971.

A mother's account of her very brilliant son from infancy through his graduation from the University of Michigan at age fourteen is given.

Hall, E.G., and Skinner, Nancy. *Somewhere to turn: Strategies for parents of the gifted and talented.* New York: Teachers College Press, 1980.

Practical suggestions for parents are developed in this book. Ideas on how to determine if you have a gifted child and what parents can do on their own to help are discussed. The uses of resources beyond the home are delineated.

Hauck, B., and Freehill, M. *The gifted—case studies.* Dubuque, Iowa: Wm. C. Brown, Group, 1972.

Various individual differences within the gifted population are examined through individual case studies. Characteristics, needs, and problems of gifted individuals are emphasized.

Hegeman, K. *Gifted children in the regular classroom: The complete guide for teachers and administrators.* New York: Trillium Press, 1981.

Included in this volume are ideas for specific teaching strategies for differentiating instruction, evaluation of pupil progress, and individual education plans. A wide variety of forms and record sheets is provided.

Heimberger, M. *Teaching the gifted and talented in the elementary classroom.* Washington, D.C.: National Education Association, 1980.

Practical suggestions in reading and language arts, social studies, math, and science are offered for teaching the gifted in the elementary classroom.

Hersey, J. *The child buyer.* New York: Alfred A. Knopf, 1960.

A novel depicting mock hearings before a Senate Committee concerned with the investigation of the proposed purchase of a male child with superior intelligence is given.

Heuer, J., Koprowicz, A., and Harris, R. *Magic kits.* Mansfield Center, Conn.: Creative Learning Press, 1980.

A variety of thinking skills, including productive thinking, brainstorming, and higher cognitive processes, are integrated into many subject areas.

Heuer, J., Koprowicz, A., and Harris, R. *More magic kits.* Mansfield Center, Conn.: Creative Learning Press, 1982.

This expansion of *Magic Kits* contains additional subject areas such as architecture, consumerism, careers, and fashion.

Hildreth, G. *Introduction to the gifted.* New York: McGraw-Hill, 1966.

A survey of the gifted and their educational needs, which describes identification, administrative arrangements, creativity, educational methodologies, and teachers of the gifted is the major purpose of this book.

Hill, M. *Enrichment programs for gifted/talented pupils.* Ventura, Calif.: National/State Leadership Training Institute, Office of the Ventura County Superintendent of Schools, 1982.

In this reprint of an earlier work, the author discusses such topics as objectives and resources for enrichment. The development and examples of creative expression, critical appreciation, and the scientific approach are given.

Hitchfield, E. *In search of promise: A long-term national study of able children and their families.* Atlantic Highlands, N.J.: Humanities Press, 1974.

This is a report focusing on the attitudes of parents, teachers, and students toward the gifted. Some case studies are contained in this British Cohort study. The results of various types of tests used with these gifted students and the intercorrelations are presented.

Hollingworth, L. *Children above 180 I.Q. Stanford-Binet: Origins and development.* Salem, N.H.: Ayer Co., 1975.

Case studies of several highly precocious children studied by the author in the first half of this century are presented.

Hopkins, L., and Shapiro, A. *Creative activities for the gifted child.* Belmont, Calif.: Pitman Learning, 1969.

Enrichment ideas in art, math, music, physical education, and language arts are presented to assist the regular classroom teacher with gifted students in her classroom.

Hoyt, K., and Hebeler, J. *Career education for gifted and talented students.* Salt Lake City, Utah: Olympus Publishing, 1974.

An overview of career education for the gifted with emphasis on the current status of programs, specific needs of the gifted in career education, and a summary of national exemplary programs is set forth.

Jackson, D. (Ed.) *Readings in gifted and talented education.* Guilford, Conn.: Special Learning Corp., 1978.

General topics in the education of the gifted and talented are discussed, including curriculum, methodology, programming, and creativity.

Jackson, D. (Ed.) *Readings in curriculum development for the gifted.* Guilford, Conn.: Special Learning Corp., 1980.

Readings contained in this book focus on four areas: curriculum planning and evaluation; screening and identification; program examples; and teacher preparation and community involvement.

Jackson, D. (Ed.) *Readings in foundations of gifted education.* Guilford, Conn.: Special Learning Corp., 1980.

The four major topics addressed in this book of readings are: theoretical bases of intervention; identification; problems in evaluating special programs; and building professional and public support for the gifted.

Jay, E. *Library media projects for the gifted.* Hamden, Conn.: Shoe String Press, 1983.

Numerous activities for gifted elementary students are presented. Each requires the use of reference tools such as indexes, atlases, and specialized dictionaries.

Jenkins, R. *A resource guide to preschool and primary programs for the gifted and talented.* Mansfield Center, Conn.: Creative Learning Press, 1979.

Descriptions of sixty early childhood programs are provided. Information is given on identification, organizational patterns, and enrichment activities.

Johnson, B. (Ed.) *New directions for gifted education.* Ventura, Calif.: National/State Leadership Training Institute, Office of the Ventura County Superintendent of Schools, 1976.

This report of the bicentennial midyear Leadership Training Institute contains presentations by Frank Barron, Delmo Della-Dora, Ray Ewing, Norman Hall, Robert Pearman, Don Severson, and Mary Hunter Wolfe. Topics include creativity, public awareness, program innovations, leadership, guidance, and the performing and visual arts.

Jordan, J.B., and Grossi, J.A. (Eds.) *An administrator's handbook on designing programs for the gifted and talented.* Reston, Va.: Council for Exceptional Children, 1980.

Contained in this handbook are articles on various aspects of programming for the gifted and talented, including needs assessment, budgeting, staffing, and resources. Suggestions are given on the principles of differentiated instruction, screening and identification, materials selection, and program evaluation.

Kanigher, H. *Everyday enrichment for gifted children at home and school.* Ventura, Calif.: National/State Leadership Training Institute, Office of the Ventura County Superintendent of Schools, 1977.

A variety of enrichment ideas for teachers and parents of the gifted is presented for all the major curricula areas.

Kaplan, S. *Providing programs for the gifted and talented: A handbook.* Ventura, Calif.: National/State Leadership Training Institute, Office of the Ventura County Superintendent of Schools, 1975.

Models for program development, curricula adaptations and inservice for teachers for specialized education of the gifted are outlined.

Kaplan, S. *Curricula for the gifted.* Ventura, Calif.: National/State Leadership Training Institute, Office of the Ventura County Superintendent of Schools, 1982.

This book of proceedings on the first national conference on curricula for the gifted/talented covers such topics as compacting, differentiating, and evaluation. Curriculum development for the culturally different is addressed.

Kaplan, S., et al. *Inservice training manual: Activities for identification/program planning for the gifted/talented.* Ventura, Calif.: National/State Leadership Training Institute, Office of the Superintendent of Schools, 1979.

Forms covering needs assessment, inservice plans, and an evaluative questionnaire are given. Topics discussed include differentiated curricula, instructional strategies, individualized instruction, and evaluation.

Karnes, F.A., and Collins, E.C. *Assessment in gifted education.* Springfield, Ill.: Charles C. Thomas, Publisher, 1981.

This book contains a comprehensive compilation and analysis of instruments useful in the assessment of gifted and talented students and of programs for such students. Instruments described include those on achievement, careers, cognitive development, counseling, creativity, English, foreign language, intelligence, interest, leadership, learning styles, mathematics, personality, science, self-concept, social studies, values, and visual and performing arts.

Karnes, F., and Collins, E. *Handbook of instructional resources and references for teaching the gifted.* Newton, Mass.: Allyn and Bacon, 1980.

A guide to selecting instructional materials is presented. A listing of materials appropriate for the gifted at the elementary and junior high levels is given. Annotated selected professional references are included.

Karnes, F.A., and Peddicord, H.Q. *Programs, leaders, consultants, and other resources in gifted and talented education.* Springfield, Ill.: Charles C. Thomas, Publishers, 1980.

Twenty-four preschool, elementary, and secondary programs for the gifted and talented are discussed. National leaders and state consultants in gifted education are highlighted. In addition, a listing of resource persons by state, with their areas of expertise, is provided.

Karnes, M. *The underserved: Our young gifted children.* Reston, Virginia: The Council for Exceptional Children, 1983.

This guide to the development of the young gifted contains information on identification, characteristics, and affective development. Instructional models, differentiated curriculum, and program evaluation are discussed.

Kaufman, F. *Your gifted child and you.* Reston, Va.: Council for Exceptional Children, 1976.

Practical suggestions for parents to develop creativity and help their gifted children develop their interests are the major focus. Suggestions for developing parent organizations and a national list of parent organizations for the gifted are included.

Keating, D. (Ed.) *Intellectual talent: Research and development.* Baltimore, Md.: Johns Hopkins University Press, 1976.

Several authors relate to the general needs of the gifted. In addition, articles focus on the mathematically gifted and the work of Julian Stanley and others at Johns Hopkins University.

Keating, D., and Stanley, J. *From eighth grade to selected college in one jump: Case studies in radical acceleration.* Baltimore, Md.: Johns Hopkins University Press, 1972.

This is a report on the acceleration of highly gifted adolescents into college programs. The negative and positive consequences of acceleration are enumerated.

Kemnitz, T., Patterson, S., and Zerman, S. *From pirates to astronauts.* New York: Trillium Press, 1980.

This book contains open-ended stories and activities pertaining to American history for gifted students in grades three through seven. Books for research and further study are listed.

Keyes, F. *Exploring careers for the gifted.* New York: Richards Rosen Press, 1981.

Topics discussed in career education for the gifted include careers of the future and how to select your school and college. Recommended career specialties are cited in a wide variety of academic fields.

Khatena, J. *Educational psychology of the gifted.* New York: John Wiley and Sons, 1982.

The nature and types of giftedness as well as ways of identification are delineated. The intellectual and creative development of the students, along with the problems they face, are discussed. Support services and agencies are given.

Kough, J. *Practical programs for the gifted.* Chicago: Science Research Associates, 1960.

Sequential steps needed in establishing and administering a school program for gifted students are treated in this book.

Kramer, A. H. (Ed.) *Gifted children: Challenging their potential—new perspectives and alternatives.* New York: Trillium Press, 1981.

The proceedings from the Third International Conference on Gifted and Talented held in Jerusalem in 1979 contain thirty-three articles. Topics on the nature and nurturing of giftedness, curriculum alternatives, and the culturally diverse gifted are included.

Krueger, M. *On being gifted.* New York: Walker, 1978.

The book is a compilation of statements by gifted students on their perceptions of the world in which they live. Remarks focus on self, family, school, important persons in their lives, and their futures.

Laubenfels, J. *The gifted student: An annotated bibliography.* Westport, Conn.: Greenwood Press, 1977.

This is an annotated compilation of articles pertinent to the gifted, selected from professional journals, books, conference reports, dissertations, government documents, and pamphlets. Articles included focus on general information, identification techniques, educational programming, special problems, and related research.

Lawless, R. *A guide for educating a gifted child in your classroom.* Buffalo, N.Y.: Disseminators of Knowledge Publishers, 1976.

Fundamental information on gifted students is presented in an easily readable format which is particularly pertinent for regular classroom teachers. Characteristics, problems, identification techniques, and curricular adaptations for gifted students are covered.

Lawless, R. *Programs for gifted/talented/creative children.* Buffalo, N.Y.: Disseminators of Knowledge Publishers, 1977.

An overview of program planning considerations, selected program descriptions, and curriculum applications are presented in basic terminology. Learning activities for gifted students are also provided.

Laycock, F. *Gifted children.* Glenview, Ill.: Scott, Foresman, 1979.

The author addresses topics in gifted education such as characteristics, identification, and educational practices at the national and international levels. Also, current problems and issues in gifted education are discussed.

Laycock, S. *Gifted children: A handbook for the classroom teacher.* Toronto: Copp Clark Pitman, 1957.

Specific methods for teaching gifted students in the major curricular areas are discussed for the regular education teacher at the elementary and secondary levels.

Lewis, C., Buckley, S., and Meseroll, C. *GEMINI: Gifted education manual for individualizing networks of instruction.* New York: Trillium Press, 1980.

Six process areas are detailed. The four within the cognitive classification are independent study, critical thinking, creativity, and communication. Personal growth and motivational development are the two within the affective domain.

Maker, C.J. *Curriculum development for the gifted.* Rockville, Md.: Aspen Systems Corp., 1982.

Modifications in content, process, product, and the learning environment for the gifted are discussed. Program examples are given for an early childhood program, elementary resource room program, a partially self-contained middle school program, and a high school seminar program.

Maker, C.J. *Teaching models in education of the gifted.* Rockville, Md.: Aspen Systems Corp., 1982.

Ten teaching models are detailed, including assumptions underlying each, advantages and disadvantages of using each with the gifted, and ways of modifying the approaches. Research on the effectiveness is discussed, and resources and teaching materials are given.

Maker, C.J. *Training teachers for the gifted and talented: A comparison of models.* Reston, Va.: Council for Exceptional Children, 1975.

Various program plans for preservice and inservice training of teachers of the gifted and talented are compared. Characteristics of teachers of the gifted are delineated.

Maker, C.J. *Providing programs for the gifted handicapped.* Reston, Va.: Council for Exceptional Children, 1977.

This book contains practical suggestions for programming with emphasis on ways of conducting programs for this unique group of individuals. A resource guide and directory of programs are included.

Mallis, J. *Diamonds in the dust: Discover and develop your child's gifts*. Austin, Tex.: Multi Media Arts, 1983.

This book is an activity text, which is designed to be used with a child to identify and stimulate potential abilities in all areas of giftedness. It can be utilized with all age groups.

Mallis, J. (Ed.) *Ideas for teaching gifted students*. Austin, Tex.: Multi Media Arts, 1980.

This series of eight books focuses on the following areas: visual arts, science, English, mathematics, music, language arts, and social studies at the elementary and secondary levels. Objectives, activities, and resources are given for each area.

Mallis, J., et al. *Reaching for the stars: A minicourse for education of gifted students*. Austin, Tex.: Multi Media Arts, 1979.

This series of ten books is designed to be used in preservice and inservice training. The following topics are addressed for the gifted and talented: characteristics, needs, underachievers, handicapped, disadvantaged, intelligence, creativity, enrichment, programs, and guidance and counseling. In each booklet, selected references and readings are given.

Marland, S. *Education of the gifted and talented: Report to the subcommittee on education, committee on labor and public welfare, United States Senate*. Washington, D.C.: United States Government Printing Office, 1972.

Following the mandate of P.L. 91-230, this former Commissioner of Education presented to Congress this report on the gifted and talented which included a proposed definition, needs, present status of programs, and testimony underscoring the most critical areas of gifted education.

Martinson, R. *Curriculum enrichment for the gifted in the primary grades*. Englewood Cliffs, N.J.: Prentice-Hall, 1968.

Techniques are described which can enable the elementary classroom teacher to meet the interests and needs of individual gifted children in the regular school program. Special provisions for curriculum planning are treated for music, art, language arts, science, math, and social studies.

Martinson, R. *A guide toward better teaching for the gifted.* Ventura, Calif.: National/State Leadership Training Institute, Office of the Ventura County Superintendent of Schools, 1976.

Primarily directed at teachers of the gifted, this book covers such topics as curriculum planning, data collection, rating scales, and teacher preparation.

Martinson, R. *The identification of the gifted and talented.* Ventura, Calif.: National/State Leadership Training Institute, Office of the Ventura County Superintendent of Schools, 1973.

A variety of suggestions for the screening and identification of the gifted and talented are set forth and critiqued. Identification materials used by various school agencies are included.

Martinson, R., and Seagoe, M. *The abilities of young children.* Reston, Va.: Council for Exceptional Children, 1967.

A study to determine the relationship between intelligence and creativity and to establish criteria for evaluating the creative products of elementary students is described.

Mass, L. *Kids working with kids.* New York: Trillium Press, 1980.

This book is a guide for teachers to use in helping students to work independently on projects, to work with younger children, and to assist handicapped students. Various forms and charts are included.

Miles, W.R. (Ed.) *Research and issues in gifted and talented education: Implications for teacher education.* Washington, D.C.: ERIC Clearinghouse on Teacher Education, 1981.

This compilation of papers includes such topics as: the teacher's role in identification; math for gifted girls; guidance for the gifted; and goals, programs, and evaluation.

Miley, J., et al. *Promising practices: Teaching the disadvantaged gifted.* Ventura, California: National/State Leadership Training Institute, Office of the Ventura County Superintendent of Schools, 1975.

Several authorities in the field of culturally different gifted address themselves to culture diversity and giftedness, creativity among different cultures, and giftedness in females.

Miller, B.S., and Price, M. *The gifted child, the family, and the community.* New York: Walker, 1981.

A compendium of articles for and about parents of gifted children. Contains information on family relationships, community resources, school programs, and additional options for the gifted.

Mitchell, P. (Ed.) *A policymaker's guide to issues in gifted and talented education.* Washington, D.C.: National Association of State Boards of Education, 1981.

Outlined are four basic steps in developing policies for educational programs for the gifted and talented. Policies and programs are described in detail for seven states and a general overview is given for the remaining states.

Mitchell, P. (Ed.) *An advocate's guide to building support for gifted and talented education.* Washington, D.C.: National Association of State Boards of Education, 1981.

Suggestions for advocacy include ideas on organizing local groups to give testimony at the local and state levels. Ideas for working with administrators, legislators, and board members are given.

Morgan, H.J., Tennant, C.G., and Gold, M.J. *Elementary and secondary level programs for the gifted and talented.* New York: Teachers College Press, 1980.

Discussed in this book are initial steps in program development, developing a written plan, selecting the organizational structure, and developing the curriculum. In addition, programs feasible for communities of various sizes and a wide range of program alternatives are set forth.

Neuman, E. *Reaching out: Advocacy for the gifted and talented.* New York: Teachers College Press, 1980.

Many aspects of advocacy are discussed, including the initial steps to be taken in organizing a group as well as ideas on ways of keeping the organization viable. A case study on a national advocacy association is presented, along with samples of local association development materials.

Oden, M. *The fulfillment of promise: 40 year follow-up of the Terman gifted group.* Stanford, Calif.: Stanford University Press, 1968.

A seventh survey of the Terman subjects was undertaken in 1960-61. The focal point of this study was a comparison of the most successful and least successful men, with differences centering on completion of college and emotional and social factors.

Olivero, J., and Sato, I. *PAB Conference report and follow-up*. Ventura, Calif.: National/State Leadership Training Institute, Office of the Ventura County Superintendent of Schools, 1975.

This report of the Parents, Administrators, and Board members conferences held in Maryland and California includes recommendations for various program developments for the gifted and talented.

Passow, A.H. *Education for gifted children and youth*. Ventura, Calif.: National/State Leadership Training Institute, Office of the Ventura County Superintendent of Schools, 1981.

This book contains a collection of selected articles and papers published between 1956 and 1962. Topics include ability grouping, enrichment, underachievement, and social education.

Passow, A.H. (Ed.) *The gifted and the talented: Their education and development*. Chicago: National Society for the Study of Education, 1979.

The Seventy-eighth Yearbook of the National Society for the Study of Education contains a historical overview of gifted education in addition to articles focusing on educational policies, programs, and practices for typical as well as atypical groups of gifted and talented children and adults.

Perino, S., and Perino, J. *Parenting the gifted: Developing the promise*. New York: R.R. Bowker, 1981.

Guidance for parents focuses on such topics as ways to identify the gifted, and appropriate tests to use in the process, information on enrichment and acceleration, and special problems of gifted adolescents. A glossary of terms and a selected bibliography are included.

Perrone, P.A., and Male, R.A. *Developmental education and guidance of talented learners*. Rockville, Md.: Aspen Systems Corp., 1981.

The needs and the development of talented students are described. Programs to enhance their potential and capabilities are detailed.

Plowman, P. *Teaching the gifted and talented in the social studies classroom.* Washington, D.C.: National Education Association, 1980.

This guide to social studies for the gifted contains sample units and discussion on strategies to enhance a variety of thinking skills in this academic area.

Polette, N. *Picture books for gifted programs.* Metuchen, N.J.: Scarecrow Press, 1981.

Picture books and Piaget's theory are discussed. Books appropriate to communication skills, productive thinking, and critical thinking for the gifted are described.

Polette, N. *3 R's for the gifted: Reading, writing and research.* Littleton, Colo.: Libraries Unlimited, 1982.

Twelve learning modules are given in the areas of literature, reading/writing skills, science, and social studies. Numerous activities are suggested for each area.

Polette, N., and Hamlin, M. *Exploring books with the gifted.* Littleton, Colo.: Libraries Unlimited, 1980.

Objectives and a variety of activities are given for the use of books with the gifted. References are also provided.

Povey, R.M. (Ed.) *Educating the gifted child.* London: Harper & Row, 1980.

This compilation of articles from Great Britain focuses on the research and the practices in the education of gifted children and techniques and strategies in helping the gifted. Individual case studies of gifted youth are included.

Pringle, M. *Able misfits: A study of educational and behavior difficulties of 103 very intelligent children, I.Q.'s 120-200.* Atlantic HIghlands, N.J.: Humanities Press, 1971.

Characteristics, backgrounds, and behavioral manifestations of a group of gifted children with behavioral disorders are analyzed. Early recognition of giftedness is emphasized.

Ray, J. *Turning on bright minds—A parent looks at gifted education in Texas.* Menlo Park, Calif.: Prologues, 1977.

The history of gifted education in Texas with a comprehensive overview of current status and development of programs is presented. Locations and types of programs are detailed. A listing of organizations and associations completes this publication.

Reid, C., and Reid, J. *SOAR: A program for the gifted, Parent's guidebook.* Rolling Hills Estates, Calif.: B.L. Winch and Associates, 1982.

A book for parents designed to assist them in incorporating higher level thinking skills in the home.

Reid, C., and Reid, J. *SOAR: A program for the gifted using Bloom's Taxonomy, Teacher's guidebook.* Rolling Hills Estates, Calif.: B.L. Winch and Associates, 1982.

Information and activities based on Bloom's Taxonomy for the teacher to incorporate into the instructional process is presented.

Renzulli, J. *The enrichment triad model: A guide for developing defensible programs for the gifted and talented.* Mansfield Center, Conn.: Creative Learning Press, 1977.

Included are various approaches to enrichment, instruments for identifying students' interests, techniques for identifying community resources, and a list of enrichment activities particularly suitable for the gifted.

Renzulli, J. *A guidebook for evaluating programs for the gifted and talented.* Ventura, Calif.: National/State Leadership Training Institute on the Gifted and Talented, Office of the Ventura County Superintendent of Schools, 1975.

Practical suggestions for evaluating programs for the gifted which are based on input from students, parents, teachers, administrators, and other concerned individuals are the major focus of this book. Sample copies of evaluation forms are provided.

Renzulli, J. and Smith, L. *A guidebook for developing individualized educational programs for gifted and talented students.* Mansfield Center, Conn.: Creative Learning Press, 1979.

The authors present an overview of the purposes and design of individual education plans and extend this to a discussion of such plans for gifted students. Specific techniques and instruments are described for assessing individual strengths and learning styles. Methods for utilizing such information in educational programming are explained.

Renzulli, J. *What makes giftedness?* Ventura, Calif.: National/State Leadership Training Institute, Office of the Ventura County Superintendent of Schools, 1979.

Various definitions of gifted/talented are discussed, including the three-ring conception by the author. Types of information used in identification systems are examined.

Renzulli, J., Reis, S., and Smith, L. *The revolving door identification model.* Mansfield Center, Conn.: Creative Learning Press, 1981.

The theory and implementation of the revolving door model are set forth. Many forms and suggestions for school personnel are presented.

Renzulli, J., and Smith, L. *A guidebook for developing individualized educational programs for gifted and talented students.* Mansfield Center, Conn.: Creative Learning Press, 1979.

An overview of the IEP model and ways to assess student strengths are given. Procedures for compacting the regular curriculum and directions for developing management plans for individual and small group investigations are included.

Renzulli, J.S., and Stoddard, E.P. *Gifted and talented education in perspective.* Reston, Va.: Council for Exceptional Children, 1980.

Articles from *Exceptional Children* and *Teaching Exceptional Children* are arranged thematically. Topics include identification, characteristics, culturally different, curriculum, research, and programs.

Reynolds, M. (Ed.) *Early school admission for mentally advanced children.* Reston, Va.: Council for Exceptional Children, 1962.

This series of articles reviews early school admission as a programming alternative for gifted students. Pertinent issues and possible negative and positive consequences are discussed.

Rice, J. *The gifted: Developing total talent.* Springfield, Ill.: Charles C. Thomas, Publisher, 1970.

Organizational and administrative concerns in program development for the gifted are the focal point of this text. Included are sections on the historical aspects, a model for talent classification, identification, procedures, programming alternatives, and curriculum models.

Rivlin, H. *Advantage: Disadvantaged gifted.* Ventura, Calif.: National/State Leadership Training Institute on the Gifted and Talented, Office of the Ventura County Superintendent of Schools, 1978.

Synopses of presentations from the Third National Conference on the Disadvantaged Gifted, in addition to other related articles, are contained within this volume. Various articles are pertinent to the educational needs of gifted black, Spanish-speaking, female, economically deprived, rural, Asian, and Native Americans.

Roedell, W.C., Jackson, N.E., and Robinson, H.B. *Gifted young children.* New York: Teachers College Press, 1980.

Discussed in this volume, written specifically about young gifted children, are such topics as early identification, characteristics, and programs. Descriptions of sample programs are provided.

Roomey, W. *Teaching the gifted and talented in the science classroom.* Washington, D.C.: National Education Association, 1980.

The author describes the characteristics of the gifted and what makes a gifted scientist. Sample activities for teaching science to the gifted are described.

Rubenzer, R. *Educating the other half: Implications of left/right brain research.* Reston, Va.: Council for Exceptional Children, 1982.

Contained in this book are a review and synthesis of research on the topic. Thirty-five classroom activities designed to stimulate integrated right brain processes are given.

Runions, T. *Stewardship: Training the gifted as community mentors.* Reston, Va.: Council for Exceptional Children, 1982.

Steps and examples in establishing a stewardship program are given. Forms and checklists to be used in program implementation are provided.

Sanderlein, O. *Teaching gifted children.* San Diego, Calif.: A.S. Barnes, 1973.

Current needs in gifted education are explored from a national perspective. Descriptions of model gifted programs throughout the United States are outlined.

Sato, I., Birnbaum, M., and LoCicero, J. *Developing a written plan for the education of gifted and talented students.* Ventura, Calif.: National/State Leadership Training Institute, Office of the Ventura County Superintendent of Schools, 1974.

A matrix encompasses the major factors in program planning which includes position statement, planning tasks, goals, objectives, programs, budgetary considerations, and strategies for change. These elements are detailed to assist superintendents and local administrators in the development of programs for the gifted.

Sato, I. (Ed.) *Balancing the scale for the disadvantaged gifted.* Ventura, Calif.: National/State Leadership Training Institute, Office of the Ventura County Superintendent of Schools, 1981.

Presentations from the fourth national conference on disadvantaged gifted and talented are given. Identification, developing potential, developing programs, and training teachers are discussed.

Sellin, D., and Birch, J. *Educating gifted and talented leaners.* Rockville, Md.: Aspen Systems Corp., 1980.

Special needs of the handicapped and disabled gifted student, as well as the characteristics and needs of the more typical student in this classification, are discussed. In addition, ways of evaluating programs for these outstanding youth are given.

Sellin, D., and Birch, J. *Psychoeducational development of gifted and talented learners.* Rockville, Md.: Aspen Systems Corp., 1981.

The understanding of various approaches to social development of human abilities is discussed. Suggestions for models of quality programs and for individualizing instruction are given.

Smith, L. (Ed.) *The Triad prototype series: Curriculum units for the gifted and talented based upon the enrichment triad model.* Mansfield Center, Conn.: Creative Learning Press, 1978.

This series includes three booklets dealing with the topics of lunchroom waste, entomology, and Victorian architecture. A completed Management Plan for Individual and Small Group Investigations is included for each subject.

Smith, L. (Ed.) *The Triad prototype series: Curriculum units for the gifted and talented based upon the enrichment triad model.* Mansfield Center, Conn.: Creative Learning Press, 1980.

Four booklets are included in this series. The topics are civil defense, genealogy, cartoon art, and Shakespeare.

Stanley, J., George, W., and Solano, C. (Eds.) *The gifted and the creative: A fifty-year perspective.* Baltimore, Md.: Johns Hopkins University Press, 1977.

This is a compilation of eight essays presented at the Seventh Annual Hyman Blumberg Symposium on Research in Early Childhood Education. The topics include: history of gifted education, sex differences in regard to program planning, mathematically precocious youth, disadvantaged gifted children, personality attributes of the gifted, and articles relevant to the Terman studies.

Stanley, J., George, W., and Solano, C. (Eds.) *The gifted and creative.* Baltimore, Md.: Johns Hopkins University Press, 1978.

Trends in the education of the gifted and the results of a logitudinal study of three thousand mathematically talented youth are presented and discussed.

Stanley, J., George, W., and Solano, C. *Educational programs and intellectual prodigies.* Baltimore, Md.: Johns Hopkins University Press, 1978.

Published as a supplement to *The Gifted and the Creative: A Fifty Year Perspective,* this monograph contains additional papers focusing on programs for the gifted and talented and profiles of intellectual prodigies. Programs described include those in California, Florida, New Jersey, Wisconsin, and Maryland.

Stanley, J., Keating, D., and Fox, L. (Eds.) *Mathematical talent: Discovery, description, and development.* Baltimore, Md.: Johns Hopkins University Press, 1974.

The identification of and educational programming for these students are set forth and discussed. Suggestions for assisting mathematically talented youth in our current educational system are given.

Stewart, E., and Dean, M. *The almost whole earth catalog of process oriented enrichment materials.* Mansfield Center, Conn.: Creative Learning Press, 1980.

Process learning materials for academic areas and how-to-do books in a wide variety of areas are listed. Publisher, cost, and a description are given for each.

Stoltz, B., and Saloom, P. *The why, what, and how of interest development centers.* Mansfield Center, Conn.: Creative Learning Press, 1977.

Detailed descriptions on how to design learning centers are the focus of the book. Diagrams, materials, and resources are included.

Strang, R. *Helping your gifted child.* New York: E.P. Dutton, 1960.

The major focus of this book is upon the role of the parent in the educational development of gifted children from preschool to the secondary level.

Sumption, M., and Luecking, M. *Education of the gifted.* New York: Ronald Press, 1960.

A comprehensive overview of all aspects of gifted education, including an historical overview, role of the community, and college programs is given.

Syphers, D. *Gifted and talented: Practical programming for teachers and principals.* Reston, Va.: Council for Exceptional Children, 1972.

Practical suggestions for administrators and teachers on programming for the gifted and talented are discussed.

Tannenbaum, A. *Gifted children: Psychological and educational perspectives.* New York: Macmillan, 1983.

The history of giftedness and issues in its definition are given. A review of underachievement as well as creativity is discussed. In addition, information on nurturing high potential with a discussion on a proposed enrichment matrix is provided.

Tempest, N. *Teaching clever children: 7–11.* Boston: Routledge and Kegan Paul of America, 1974.

Based on a study of gifted children in England, the author sets forth numerous suggestions for teaching methods for young gifted students. The book is divided into sections on types of thinking processes, rather than subject matter areas.

Terman, L., and Oden, M. *Genetic studies of genius. Volume V, The gifted group at mid-life.* Stanford, Calif.: Stanford University Press, 1957.

This later folow-up study focuses on the gifted subjects at mid-life (middle forties), thirty-five years after the original investigation. Additional information is presented on mortality, health, avocational interests, political and social attitudes, marriage, divorce, income, and offspring.

Terman, L., et al. *Genetic studies of genius. Volume I, Mental and physical traits of a thousand gifted children.* Stanford, Calif.: Stanford University Press, 1925.

This initial volume of the series contains and describes the results of data collected on the backgrounds, mental and physical traits, and attitudes of over one thousand children (I.Q. above 140) included in this longitudinal study on gifted individuals.

Terman, L., et al. *Genetic studies of genius. Volume IV, The gifted child grows up.* Stanford, Calif.: Stanford University Press, 1947.

This volume reports the results of follow-up studies on the subjects in the original study of gifted children begun in 1921. Information is presented on their educational histories, vocational choices, and personal and social adjustment.

Thomas, G., and Crescimbeni, J. *Guiding the gifted child.* New York: Random House, 1966.

The central focus of this book is upon the identification of gifted students and upon diverse arrangements for program and curriculum planning. Some attention is given to the characteristics of the gifted and to the guidance of gifted students.

Torrance, E.P. *Discovery and nurturance of giftedness in the culturally different.* Reston, Va.: Council for Exceptional Children, 1977.

Strategies and techniques for identifying the gifted and talented among the culturally different are provided. Sample checklists are included as well as an annotated bibliography.

Torrance, E.P. *Gifted children in the classroom.* New York: Macmillan, 1966.

This book is a practical treatise on the education of the gifted child for teachers and administrators. In addition to the topics of identification and curriculum development, the author gives practical suggestions for working with gifted children in the kindergarten and for developing creative reading skills in gifted children.

Treffinger, D. *Blending gifted education with the total school program.* Williamsville, N.Y.: Center for Creative Learning, 1981.

This handbook describes individualized programming for the gifted with emphasis on the total school program. Included are worksheets, inventories, and resources for inservice staff development.

Treffinger, D., and Curl, C. *Self-directed study guide on the education of the gifted and the talented.* Ventura, Calif.: National/State Leadership Training Institute on the Gifted and Talented, Office of the Ventura County Superintendent of Schools, 1977.

This work provides a resource to undertake an in-depth self study on the gifted, talented, and creative. Pre- and post-self assessments with numerous bibliographical sources to journals and texts are furnished.

Tuttle, F. *Gifted and talented students.* Washington, D.C.: National Education Association, 1978.

Research is reviewed and summarized in the areas of characteristics, identification, program design, teacher selection and evaluation in gifted education.

Tuttle, F., and Becker, L. *Characteristics and identification of gifted and talented students.* Washington, D.C.: National Education Association, 1980.

Characteristics and identification of the gifted and talented are discussed through three components of the book: overview and background, supplementary materials, and activities.

Tuttle, F., and Becker, L. Program design and development for gifted and talented students. Washington, D.C.: National Education Association, 1980.

The major components of this book on program development are rationale, curricular models, administrative design, evaluation, and teacher selection.

Vail, P.L. *The world of the gifted child.* New York: Walker, 1979.

The needs, characteristics, and problems of gifted persons and their families are related in a personal manner. Techniques for recognizing giftedness are presented, and a discussion of handicapped gifted children is included. Suggestions are provided for parents and teachers.

Van Tassel-Baska, J. (Ed.) *A practical guide to counseling the gifted in a school setting.* Reston, Virginia: The Council for Exceptional Children, 1983.

This guide for professionals without special training in guidance contains information on the affective differences of gifted students and ways that parents and others can encourage and assist development.

Van Tassel-Baska, J. *An administrator's guide to the education of gifted and talented children.* Washington, D.C.: National Association of State Boards of Education, 1981.

The necessary steps for beginning a program or changing a program for the gifted are detailed in this book. In addition, key issues in program development are discussed.

Vezza, T., and Bagley, M. *The investigation of real problems: A teacher's handbook for developing higher level thinking skills in gifted and talented children.* Woodcliff Lake, N.J.: New Dimensions for the 80's Publishers, 1979.

Objectives and research questions are given in a wide variety of topics, including crime, health, ecology, economics, space, genealogy, food, and media. References from local and school libraries, industries, agencies, and individuals are cited.

Ward, V. *Educating the gifted, an axiomatic approach.* Columbus, Ohio: Charles E. Merrill, Publishing, 1961.

Curriculum is examined for teachers, administrators, and other supervisory personnel concerned with the education of the gifted. A comprehensive checklist for instructional provisions is an integral feature.

Ward, V. *Differential education for the gifted.* Ventura, Calif.: National/State Leadership Training Institute, Office of the Ventura County Superintendent of Schools, 1980.

This reprint of the 1961 book by the same title includes a list of fifty studies completed by the author.

Webb, J., Meckstroth, E., and Tolan, S. *Guiding the gifted child— A practical source for parents and teachers.* Columbus, Ohio: Ohio Psychology Publishing Company, 1983.

Suggestions are offered for special problems and concerns pertaining to gifted youth. Advice on family situations, peer and sibling relationships, motivation, discipline, and stress management are given.

West, W. *Teaching the gifted and talented in the English classroom.* Washington, D.C.: National Education Association, 1980.

Characteristics of the gifted in English are discussed and language arts/English activities are offered. Suggestions for selecting unit themes are given.

Whitmore, J.R. *Giftedness, conflict and underachievement.* Newton, Mass.: Allyn and Bacon, 1980.

A comprehensive treatment of the gifted underachiever is presented. Emphasis is on definition, identification, programming, and prognosis for this unique group of gifted students.

Wolfe, D. (Ed.) *The discovery of talent.* Cambridge, Mass.: Harvard University Press, 1969.

A collection of articles emanating from the Bingham Lectures on the Development of Exceptional Abilities and Capabilities at Harvard University is brought together in this volume. These articles on superior mental capabilities focus upon inheritance, discovery, conservation, interests, recognition, environmental factors, diversity, and originality.

Wooster, J. *What to do for the gifted few.* Buffalo, N.Y.: Disseminators of Knowledge, Publishers, 1978.

Strategies for differentiating education for the gifted are presented. Ideas for meeting the cognitive and affective needs of the gifted are given and evaluation techniques are suggested.

Ziv, A. *Counseling the intellectually gifted.* New York: Teachers College Press, 1977.

Initially, background information on intellectually gifted students is presented. The second portion of the book focuses upon the role of the counselor in working with the gifted students. This latter section contains specific information on problems of gifted students and additional information on diverse types of gifted students.

ARTS, HUMANITIES, AND MUSIC

Grove, R. *The arts and the gifted: Proceedings from the national conference on arts and humanities—gifted and talented.* Reston, Va.: Council for Exceptional Children, 1975.

This is an overview of presentations at the National Conference on Arts and Humanities—Gifted and Talented. The focus is upon all aspects of the fine and performing arts for gifted and ways of implementing such programs at the local, state, and national levels.

Hickok, D., and Smith, J. *Creative teaching of music in the elementary school.* Newton, Mass.: Allyn and Bacon, 1974.

This book integrates music and the major curricula areas and suggests methods and materials for developing creativity through music.

Krueger, M., and Neuman, E. (Eds.) *Perspectives on gifted and talented: Arts and humanities.* Reston, Va.: Council for Exceptional Children, 1974.

This booklet was prepared for the National Conference on the Arts and Humanities—Gifted and Talented. It contains a directory of arts and humanities resources, an overview of arts and humanities for the gifted, and sources of federal and private funding for establishing such programs for these students.

Lowenfeld, V., and Brittain, W. *Creative and mental growth.* New York: Macmillan, 1975.

This book deals with the development of creative expression through art. The reader is assisted in understanding the art productions of students. Although the book is designed for college students and teachers, it should be of interest to parents and all others interested in the development of creative expression.

Lyon, H. *Learning to feel, feeling to learn.* Columbus, Ohio: Charles E. Merrill, Publishing, 1971.

Increased inclusion of humanistic education is advocated. A reference list including books and films is provided.

Rietson, J. *Creative teaching of art in the elementary school.* Newton, Mass.: Allyn and Bacon, 1975.

Teaching methodologies for art and for creativity are enumerated. Specific suggestions for enhancing creativity through the teaching of art are provided as well as techniques for incorporating art into the major curricula areas.

Smith, J. *Creative teaching of the creative arts in the elementary school.* Newton, Mass.: Allyn and Bacon, 1967.

Classroom strategies for the creative teaching of art, music, dance, and dramatization are explained. Practical suggestions for the regular classroom teacher are illustrated.

COMPUTERS

Ahl, D.H. *Computers in mathematics: A sourcebook of ideas.* Morristown, N.J.: Creative Computing Press, 1979.

Thinking strategies and how to solve problems, simulations, probability, computer assisted instruction, and a wide variety of programming ideas are the focus of this book of readings.

Coburn, P., et al. *Practical guide to computers in education.* Reading, Mass.: Addison-Wesley, Publishing, 1982.

Practical guidelines are discussed for selecting a computer system and educational software. Implementing a computer program in the school is detailed, and a bibliography and a listing of resources are given.

Nazarro, J.N. (Ed.) *Computer connections for gifted children and youth.* Reston, Va.: Council for Exceptional Children, 1981.

The reprints and original articles contained in this book pertain to a variety of topics in computer science, including computers in school and at home, programs, and resources. The personal experiences of gifted youth and their work with computers are related.

Papart, S. *Mindstorms: Children, computers, and powerful ideas.* New York: Basic Books, Publishers, 1980.

Described in this book is the rationale and processes in the development of LOGO, a computer assisted instructional program designed for children. The author describes experiences in implementing the program with elementary and secondary school students.

Poirot, J.L. *Computers and education.* Austin, Tex.: Sterling Swift, Publishing, 1980.

An introduction to computer assisted instruction is provided with information on computer literacy, software, and educational games. Current trends in computers in education are discussed.

Taylor, R.P. (Ed.) *The computer in the school: Tutor, tool, tutee.* New York: Teachers College Press, 1980.

This book of readings contains nineteen articles by five authorities on computers in education. Issues involved in using computers in schools, the teacher's role, and general limitations of computer use are discussed.

Thomas, J.L. (Ed.) *Microcomputers in the schools.* Phoenix, Ariz.: Oryx Press, 1981.

This book of readings details how microcomputers are being used in the schools, and what their potential may be for students, teachers, administrators, and media specialists. Many alternative uses and applications of computers in the curriculum are given.

CREATIVITY

Ainsworth-Land, V., and Fletcher, N. *Making waves with creativity problem solving.* Buffalo, N.Y.: Disseminators of Knowledge, Publishers, 1981.

Creative problem solving techniques are applied to personal problems and opportunities, classroom concerns, and subject-related situations.

Attea, M. *Turning children on through creative writing.* Buffalo, N.Y.: Disseminators of Knowledge, Publishers, 1973.

Teaching strategies for encouraging creative writing are provided, as well as suggestions for creative theory and poetry writing. Techniques for incorporating audiovisual materials are also suggested.

Bagley, M., and Hess, K. *Two hundred ways of using imagery in the classroom.* Woodcliff Lake, N.J.: New Dimensions for the 80's Publishers, 1982.

This guide for developing creativity and imagination in the classroom contains an overview of imagery and how to enhance it. Suggestions are offered in many areas of language arts, math, science, social studies, art, and music.

Barron, F. *Creative person and creative process.* New York: Holt, Rinehart and Winston, 1969.

The measurement of creativity, the relationship of intelligence and creativity, and the method for studying creative persons make up the core of this publication. Creativity and its relationship to various occupations are explored.

Biondi, A., and Parnes, S. (Eds.) *Assessing creative growth*. Great Neck, N.Y.: Creative Synergetic Associates, 1976.

Book 1 focuses on a survey of tests to measure creativity and related areas. Book 2 surveys the literature related to growth in creativity.

Callahan, C. *Developing creativity in the gifted and talented*. Reston, Va.: Council for Exceptional Children, 1978.

Strategies for teaching creativity are given for teachers. Tests used in the assessment of creativity are listed, and a general bibliography is provided.

Davis, G. *Creativity is forever*. Cross Plains, Wisc.: Badger Press, 1981.

Definitions and theories, the creative process, and tests relative to creativity are discussed. Suggestions for creative activities are given.

Davis, G., and Scott, J. *Training creative thinking*. New York: Holt, Rinehart and Winston, 1971.

The rationale, methodology, and content of creative problem solving are explained. Specific procedures for developing creative potential are suggested.

De Mille, R. *Put your mother on the ceiling*. New York: Viking Press, 1973.

Primarily written for preschool, kindergarten, and primary level teachers, this book deals with the understanding of children's imaginations. A sequence of steps is outlined to prepare the teacher for establishing imagination games and activities. Specific games are enumerated.

Eberle, B. *Visual thinking*. Buffalo, N.Y.: Disseminators of Knowledge, Publishers, 1982.

This resource book for teachers contains instructions for the development of skills in image-making, written and verbal communication, information processing, creative expression, and record keeping.

Eberle, B., and Stanish, B. *CPS for kids: A resource book for teaching creative problem solving to children.* Buffalo, N.Y.: Disseminators of Knowledge, Publishers, 1981.

This book is designed to teach the techniques of creative problem solving to children. Exercises and worksheets are provided.

Eberle, R. *Classroom cue cards for cultivating multiple talent.* Buffalo, N.Y.: Disseminators of Knowledge, Publishers, 1974.

Teaching suggestions are provided for cultivating student talent in organizing, predicting, creating, decision making, and evaluating. Also included are pupil and teacher assessment techniques and suggested methods of talent identification.

Eberle, R. *Scamper—Games for imagination and development.* Buffalo, N.Y.: Disseminators of Knowledge, Publishers, 1971.

Teachers of young children will find this to be a helpful resource book of ideas on creative thinking, creative writing, and creative games.

Farnham-Diggory, S. *Cognitive processes in education: A psychological preparation for teaching and curriculum development.* New York: Harper & Row, 1972.

Although portions of this book are not directly pertinent to gifted students, the latter part presents a discussion of the creative process. Topics covered are divergent thinking, training fluencies, the role of intelligence, personality factors and various exercises in creativity.

Feldhusen, J., et al. *Creativity research and educational planning.* Ventura, Calif.: National/State Leadership Training Institute, Office of the Ventura County Superintendent of Schools, 1982.

Selected conference proceedings address such topics as research with children and adults and several models of creative thinking and problem solving.

Feldhusen, J., and Treffinger, D. *Teaching creative thinking and problem solving.* Dubuque, Iowa: Kendall/Hunt, Publishing, 1977.

An overview of creativity, problem solving, and the special needs of the disadvantaged is presented. A list of materials and resources on creativity is supplied.

Feldman, D. (Ed.) *Developmental approaches to giftedness and creativity.* San Francisco: Jossey-Bass, Publishers, 1982.

The relationship between giftedness and creativity is discussed, and the nature of giftedness from a biological perspective is explored.

Gardner, H. *Art, mind, and creativity.* New York: Basic Books, Publishers, 1982.

Discussed are all aspects of creativity from theory to practical application. Suggestions are offered for teaching the arts in the school.

Getzels, J., and Jackson, P. *Creativity and intelligence: Explorations with gifted students.* New York: John Wiley and Sons, 1962.

Much of this work is devoted to the results of studies by the authors comparing highly intelligent children with highly creative children. An inquiry into the correlation between high intelligence and high creativity was reported.

Ghiselin, B. (Ed.) *The creative process.* New York: New American Library, 1952.

Various persons noted for their creative abilities and productions in several fields of endeavor personally relate the nature of their own creative processes.

Gowan, J. *Development of the creative individual.* San Diego, Calif.: Edits Publishers, 1972.

Based on a review of the literature on creativity and its development, the existence and sequential development of eight stages *(Periodic Developmental Stage Theory)* is postulated. Creativity and self-actualization are discussed through the linkage of developmental theory and psychology of creativity.

Gowan, J., Demos, G., and Torrance, P. *Creativity: Its educational implications.* New York: John Wiley and Sons, 1967.

A collection of readings dealing with creativity and the results of research in this area is presented. Suggestions for applying research findings in the classroom are illustrated.

Gowan, J.C., Khatena, J., and Torrance, E.P. *Creativity: Its educational implications.* Dubuque, Iowa: Kendall/Hunt Publishing, 1981.

In this collection of articles, topics include theory and policy in creativity, developmental characteristics, and identification and measurement of the creative process. Suggestions are offered for guidance counselors, teachers, and parents to understand and enhance creativity.

Gruber, H., Terrill, G., and Wertheimer, M. (Eds.) *Contemporary approaches to creative thinking.* Hawthorne, N.Y.: Aldine Publishing, 1962.

A compilation of papers presented at a symposium at the University of Colorado dealing with the process of creative thinking, conditions which foster creative thinking, and the role of conformity and creative thinking is furnished.

Guilford, J. *Intelligence, creativity, and their educational implications.* San Diego, Calif.: EDITS Publishers, 1968.

Guilford's Structure of the Intellect model, theories of creativity, and the educational implications of both are discussed.

Kagan, J. (Ed.) *Creativity and learning.* Boston: Beacon Press, 1967.

A series of theoretical and research papers on the creative process focusing upon various topics such as assessment, expression, personalities, unconscious creation, scientific views, education and the learning process, creative teacher-scholars, educational environment, the cultivation of talent, and federal support of research are presented.

Khatena, J. *Major directions in creativity research.* Reston, Va.: Council for Exceptional Children, 1975.

The present state of the art in creativity research is described, and suggestions for the direction and design of future research studies are enumerated.

Khatena, J. *The creatively gifted child: Suggestions for parents and teachers.* New York: Vantage Press, 1978.

The nature and needs of the creatively gifted child are described and discussed. Suggestions are provided that can enable parents and teachers to stimulate creative thinking.

Khatena, J. *Teaching gifted children to use creative imagination imagery.* Starkville, Miss.: Allan Associates, 1979.

Set forth in the book are ways of assisting able students to stimulate their creative imagination imagery to enhance their creative thinking. Numerous and varied activities are presented.

Khatena, J. *Creative imagination imagery actionbook.* Starkville, Miss.: Allan Associates, 1981.

Suggestions are offered for organizational strategies to facilitate creative imagination imagery. In addition, planned experiences are provided the reader on this topic.

Lytton, H. *Creativity and education.* New York: Schocken Books, 1972.

A comparison of convergent and divergent modes of thinking, creativity and intelligence assessment, the nature of the creative process, characteristics of the creative, the development of creativity, and educational implications are the topics of concern.

MacKinnon, D. *In search of human effectiveness: Identifying and developing creativity.* Great Neck, N.Y.: Creative Synergetic Associates, 1978.

Based upon scientific theory and research findings, this book treats creativity, personality factors, and personal effectiveness. The nature of creative individuals is explored and discussed in detail.

Michael, W. (Ed.) *Teaching for creative endeavor.* Bloomington: Indiana University Press, 1968.

Curriculum planning and strategies to foster creativity in a variety of areas at the elementary and secondary levels are set forth. The role of counseling and of the parents in facilitating creativity is outlined.

Mize, B. *Creative encounters.* New York: Trillium Press, 1982.

Fifty-four lessons using synectics to develop creativity in mathematics, science, history, and language arts are contained in this book.

Mooney, R., and Razik, T. (Eds.) *Explorations in creativity.* New York: Harper & Row, 1967.

A compilation of diverse papers on creativity is set forth. Topics include the nature of creativity, its development, measurement, and educational relevance.

Noller, R. *Scratching the surface of creative problem-solving.* Buffalo, N.Y.: Disseminators of Knowledge, Publishers, 1977.

The process of creative problem solving is delineated in a step-by-step approach. Illustrated examples are also given.

Parnes, S., Noller, R., and Biondi, A. *Guide to creative action.* New York: The Scribner Book Companies, 1977.

This is intended as a guidebook to the *Creative Actionbook* by the same authors. The basis is an instructional program for cultivating creative behavior. An extensive bibliography is provided.

Porterfield, G. *Kaleidoscope: Activities in creative writing and drama.* Hingham, Mass.: Teaching Resources 1978.

Activities described in creative writing include free-versa poems and story writing. Pantomime, improvisation, and play-writing are included in drama. Practice suggestions are offered for teachers and others interested in the creative nature of young persons.

Raudsepp, E. *How creative are you?* New York: Putnam Publishing Group, 1981.

The author describes the creative individual as well as barriers to creativity. Inventories for determining left/right brain orientation, values, attitudes toward work, problem solving behaviors, interests, interpersonal relations, personality dimensions, and self-perceptions are included.

Rothenberg, A., and Hausman, C. (Eds.) *The creativity question.* Durham, N.C.: Duke University Press, 1976.

A diverse collection of articles encompasses a variety of topical areas related to creativity. Included are accounts pertaining to descriptive narratives of the creative process and explanations and theories of creativity.

Sato, I. (Ed.) *The faces and forms of creativity*. Ventura, Calif.: National/State Leadership Training Institute, Office of the Ventura County Superintendent of Schools, 1981.

These are the presentations from the first conference on creativity. Topics include defining, assessing, encouraging, and applying creativity.

Schaefer, D. *Developing creativity in children*. Buffalo, N.Y.: Disseminators of Knowledge, Publishers, 1973.

A multitude of ideas is given for the development of creativity in visualization and visual arts with emphasis on prose, poetry, and dramatic expression. Suggestions for stimulating scientific thinking are also offered.

Shouksmith, G. *Intelligence, creativity, and cognitive style*. New York: John Wiley and Sons, 1970.

The emphasis of this work is upon the distinction between imaginative and logical reasoning with creativity seen as one dimension of cognitive activity. Problem solving, personality, creative thinking, and cognitive style are discussed.

Smith, J. *Setting conditions for creative teaching in the elementary school*. Newton, Mass.: Allyn and Bacon, 1966.

This book investigates the nature of creativity in its physical, psychological, educational, and social-emotional components. Suggestions are set forth for developing and nurturing creativity in all aspects of the elementary curriculum.

Taylor, C. (Ed.) *Creativity: Progress and potential*. New York: McGraw-Hill, 1964.

Various perspectives on creativity are presented, including predictive behaviors, education, development and training, and evaluation of creative production.

Taylor, I., and Getzels, J. *Perspectives in creativity*. Hawthorne, N.Y.: Aldine Publishing, 1975.

A report of conferences undertaken at the Center for Creative Leadership at Greensboro, North Carolina, is given. Contributors include Baron, Guilford, MacKinnon, Parnes, Torrance, and Taylor.

Torrance, E.P. *Creativity*. Sioux Falls, S.D.: Adapt Press, 1969.

This monograph, which is part of a series on the early learning of children, focuses upon investigations of the creative behavior of preschool and primary age children. Included are assessment techniques, the development of creative abilities, teaching activities, personality factors, and brief descriptions of famous creative persons as children.

Torrance, E.P. *Education and the creative potential.* Minneapolis: University of Minnesota Press, 1963.

A series of papers and research studies which explore creative talent from several perspectives: potential, facilitating and inhibiting factors, mental health, learning, identification, diverse cultures, and sex roles are incorporated in this publication.

Torrance, E.P. *Rewarding creative behavior.* Englewood Cliffs, N.J.: Prentice-Hall, 1965.

A plan is proposed for studying creative behavior measurement, evaluation, and rewards. Three groups of studies are presented. The first set focuses on the intermediate environment; the second upon the evaluation of others; and the final set is concerned with helping children value their ideas.

Torrance, E.P. *Encouraging creativity in the classroom.* Dubuque, Iowa: William C. Brown, Publishers, 1970.

Techniques for the development of creative abilities in the educational program are outlined, including suggestions for different subject areas. The Ideal Child Checklist is presented and explained.

Torrance, E.P. *Guiding creative talent.* Englewood Cliffs, N.J.: Prentice-Hall, 1962. (Reprint, R.E. Krieger Publishing, Melbourne, Fla., 1976.)

The identification, development, and guidance of highly creative abilities is discussed. Problems of highly creative individuals are examined. Goals to guide counselors, teachers, and administrators in the enhancement of creative talent are also included.

Torrance, E.P. *The search for satori and creativity.* Great Neck, N.Y.: Creative Synergetic Associates, 1979.

The Japanese concept of "satori," or excellence in thinking and creativity, is described in this book. Descriptions and examples of the elements of emotion, fantasy, humor, originality, and fluence in creativity are given.

Torrance, E.P., and Myers, R. *Creative learning and teaching.* New York: Harper & Row, 1970.

Teaching techniques for the enhancement of creativity are set forth. Among these are questioning for information and thought, awareness of various solutions to problems, asking provocative questions, promoting questioning in children, providing an appropriate environment, and guidance of planned sequences of creative activities.

Treffinger, D. *Encouraging creative learning for the gifted and talented.* Ventura, Calif.: National/State Leadership Training Institute, Office of the Ventura County Superintendent of Schools, 1980.

This handbook of methods and techniques sets forth ideas for a three level model of creative learning. Listings of resources are provided.

Treffinger, D., Isaksen, S., and Firestein, R. *Handbook of creative learning.* Williamsburg, N.Y.: Center for Creative Learning, 1982.

Information on the creative learning process, including definition, methodology, and examples of training exercises and activities are contained in this handbook.

Vernon, P. *Creativity.* Baltimore, Md.: Penguin Books, 1970.

This collection of readings on creativity examines major contributions of the past and present. The writings of Terman, Roe, Heinze, Stein, Poincare, Tchaikovsky, and Mozart are included. The focus is upon theoretical papers, psychometric approaches, enhancement of creativity, the relationship between creativity and personality, and personal accounts of the creative process by diverse types of creative individuals.

Wallach, M., and Kogan, N. *Modes of thinking in young children: A study of the creativity-intelligence distinction.* New York: Holt, Rinehart and Winston, 1965.

The expressed purpose of this book is twofold: (1) to investigate the hypothesis that there is a cognitive distinction between creativity and intelligence, and (2) to examine the psychological correlates of intelligence and creativity, provided that a distinction in psychological functioning could be established. Findings indicate some distinction in intellectual and creative functioning in children.

Waston, A. *What happens next?* New York: Teachers College Press, 1978.

Designed for the intermediate school student, the story starters contained in this book cover a wide variety of topics.

Whiting, C. *Creative thinking.* New York: Van Nostrand Reinhold, 1958.

The production of creative ideas is explored by examining the nature of creative thinking, steps in creative production, enhancement of creativity, and factors detrimental to creative production. Specific techniques for the development of creative thought production, such as brainstorming and the Gordon technique, are covered in detail. Although attention is given to creative production in management and business, educational programs and techniques are treated.

CRITICAL THINKING, LOGIC, AND PROBLEM SOLVING

Aschner, M., and Bish, C. *Productive thinking in education.* Washington, D.C.: National Education Association, 1965.

A compilation of papers delivered at two conferences held by the National Education Association in conjunction with their project on academically talented students is provided. Topics included: intelligence and its development; motivation, personality, and productive thinking; assessment of productive thinking; and education for productive thinking.

Aylesworth, T., and Reagan, G. *Teaching for thinking.* Garden City, N.Y.: Doubleday, 1969.

Detailed explorations of critical thinking, analysis, synthesis, logical thinking, value judgments, problem identification, hypothesis formulation and testing, deriving conclusions, and evaluation are treated in this book.

Burton, W., Kimball, R., and Wing, R. *Education for effective thinking*. New York: John Wiley and Sons, 1960.

Based upon the belief that the development of effective thinking processes should be a major goal of our educational procedures, aspects of the thinking process from goals and hypotheses to the testing of conclusions are explained. Teaching thinking skills in different subject matter areas is also treated, as well as the evaluation of critical thinking.

Crosby, N., and Marten, E. *Discovering philosophy*. Buffalo, N.Y.: Disseminators of Knowledge, Publishers, 1981.

Self-awareness, sensitivity, goal setting, and problem solving are developed through the activities set forth.

Davis, G. *Psychology of problem solving*. New York: Basic Books, Publishers, 1973.

Although the first portion of this book is theoretical in nature, the later chapters provide explanations and examples of inquiry activities, brainstorming, attribute testing, and idea checklists for solutions stimulation and imaginative problem solving. Also included are descriptions of some suggested laboratory problem-solving tasks and a bibliography of creativity assessment instruments.

Dearden, R., Hirst, P., and Peters, R. (Eds.) *Education and the development of reason*. Boston: Routledge and Kegan Paul of America, 1972.

A collection of articles by various authors on the educational process and on the development of reason is presented. Reasoning ability and its development is the major focus.

de Bono, E. *The five-day course in thinking*. New York: Basic Books, Publishers, 1967.

The reader is actively plunged into actual problem solving at the commencement of this book. Errors in thinking and suggestions for more effective thinking are an integral part of this guide. Insight thinking, sequential thinking, and strategic thinking constitute the major entries.

Drake, J.A. *Analyzing, learning, and teaching critical thinking skills*. Danville, Ill.: Interstate Printers and Publishers, 1976.

The book emphasizes the teaching aspects of critical thinking skills. Models for such are discussed, along with ways of analyzing assertions and arguments. A self-study guide is provided.

Ennis, R. *Ordinary logic.* Englewood Cliffs, N.J.: Prentice-Hall, 1969.

Intended as a background book in basic logic, this volume covers truth and validity, deductive reasoning, sentence reasoning, class reasoning, and combinations of sentence and class reasoning. Comprehension tests are provided at the end of each chapter.

Epley, T. *Models for thinking.* Ventura, Calif.: National/State Leadership Training Institute, Office of the Ventura County Superintendent of Schools, 1982.

A wide variety of models of thinking with examples of activities are provided. Selected references are given.

Freeman, D. *A new way to use your bean: Developing thinking skills in children.* New York: Trillium Press, 1981.

The book employs cooking to teach the cognitive processes of critical thinking, creative thinking, logic, and problem solving. Illustrations and forms are provided.

Greenes, C., Gregory, J., and Seymour, D. *Successful problem-solving techniques.* Palo Alto, Calif.: Creative Publications, 1974.

Written for both teachers and students, nine basic problem-solving techniques are explained. Suggestions for enhancing problem-solving abilities in students are provided for the teacher.

Heilman, I., and Larsen, S. *Now what do I do?* Buffalo, N.Y.: Disseminators of Knowledge, Publishers, 1981.

A compendium of activities focusing on the higher level thinking skills is delineated.

Hudgins, B. *Problem solving in the classroom.* New York: Macmillan, 1966.

A practical guide to fostering problem-solving techniques in the elementary classroom is given. The author addresses the role of the teacher, evaluation, and principles for promoting problem-solving behavior.

Inhelder, B., and Piaget, J. *The growth of logical thinking: From childhood to adolescence.* New York: Basic Books, Publishers, 1958.

The authors trace the development of logic by addressing three major areas: the development of propositional logic, the operational schemata of formal logic, and the structural integration of formal thought. Reasoning and logical thinking capabilities throughout the stages of cognitive development are presented.

Inhelder, B., and Piaget, J. *The early growth of logic in the child: Classification and seriation.* Atlantic Highlands, N.J.: Humanities Press, 1964.

A thorough examination of the precursors of logical thought in children, with emphasis on the sequential stage development of classification and seriation, is the content focus of this volume.

Jacobs, G. *When children think: Using journals to encourage creative thinking.* New York: Teachers College Press, 1970.

The author's account of techniques employed to develop the creative thinking processes of upper elementary children is furnished. The students recorded their new ideas in a journal. The author discusses the techniques and problems of conducting the program.

Kaufman, R. *Identifying and solving problems: A system approach.* San Diego, Calif.: University Associates, 1976.

Utilizing cartoons, charts, and diagrams, this book attempts to aid students in identifying and solving everyday problems logically and sequentially. The decision-making process is broken down into component steps. Generalizations to other problems may be made from the techniques presented.

Lucas, K., and Lucas, L. *Hometown, U.S.A.: A community of logic.* Buffalo, N.Y.: Disseminators of Knowledge, Publishers, 1981.

A companion to *Who Owns the Unicorn?* is more complex. Techniques in logic are developed through games.

Lucas, K., and Lucas, L. *Who owns the unicorn?* Buffalo, N.Y.: Disseminators of Knowledge, Publishers, 1981.

Deductive thinking skills are developed in sequence through the suggested games.

Mohan, M., and Laspada, S. *Mind stimulating activities.* Buffalo, N.Y.: Disseminators of Knowledge, Publishers, 1981.

The activities set forth are designed to stimulate searching for alternative solutions.

Noller, R., Treffinger, D., and Houseman, E. *It's a gas to be gifted.* Buffalo, N.Y.: Disseminators of Knowledge, Publishers, 1981.

The creative problem-solving techniques are applied to a simulation. Skills in perceiving new relationships and developing thinking skills are stressed.

Raths, L., Wasserman, S., Jonas, A., and Rathstein, A. *Teaching for thinking: Theory and application.* Columbus, Ohio: Charles E. Merrill, Publishing, 1967.

Thinking operations and behavioral characteristics that inhibit thinking are described. Application activities are provided for both the elementary and secondary teacher.

Rierson, J., and Claiborne, M. *Extending thinking abilities.* Buffalo, N.Y.: Disseminators of Knowledge, Publishers, 1981.

This two book series focuses on the thinking skills of perceiving, extending information, investigating, creating, and critiquing.

Ruchlis, H. *Clear thinking.* New York: Harper & Row, 1962.

A lively written book utilizing illustrations, cartoons, and problems to assist the reader in understanding logical reasoning, common errors in reasoning, and propaganda is provided.

Salmon, W. *Logic.* 2nd ed. Englewood Cliffs, N.J.: Prentice-Hall, 1973.

A general overview of logic including inductive and deductive reasoning is given. Emphasis is given to the language of logic.

Sharp, E. *Thinking is child's play.* New York: E.P. Dutton, 1969.

The book, directed to parents of young children, is a guide to thinking activities based on Piaget's model. Beginning with easier games and advancing to the more difficult, the purpose of each, the directions, and the necessary materials are given.

Strasser, B., et al. *Teaching toward inquiry*. Washington, D.C.: National Education Association, 1971.

Inquiry as a teaching method is explained and contrasted with other teaching methods. Topics related to inquiry teaching include the rationale, process, objectives, and techniques.

Swartzendruber, A. *Thinking skills that last*. Buffalo, N.Y.: Disseminators of Knowledge, Publishers, 1982.

Product oriented activities are presented in the areas of academics, creativity, arts, and leadership.

Valett, R. *Developing cognitive abilities*. St. Louis, Mo.: C.V. Mosby, 1978.

A book for teachers in which models of cognitive abilities are described and a detailed critical thinking skills survey is presented. Ideas for teaching critical and creative thinking are given.

Wadsworth, B. *Piaget for the classroom teacher*. New York: Longman, 1978.

Cognitive development is explained and its enhancement through reading, mathematics, science, and social studies instruction is described. The assessment of cognitive development, using Piagetian techniques is explained.

Wadsworth, B. *Piaget's theory of cognitive development*. New York: Longman, 1979.

Piaget's theory is summarized for the educator with detailed descriptions of each of the four levels. A bibliography is provided.

FUTURISM

Allain, V. *Futuristics and education*. Bloomington, Ind.: Phi Delta Kappa, 1979.

Selected examples of futuristics in the classroom are given for elementary, secondary, and post-secondary schools. Futuristic investigations through scenarios, science fiction, group opinion, cross-impact matrix, and simulation gaming are discussed.

Bleedorn, B. *Looking ahead: Tested ideas in future studies.* Buffalo, N.Y.: Disseminators of Knowledge, Publishers, 1981.

Creative problem solving, future wheels, a cross impact matrix, and scenario writing activities are suggested for the study of the future.

Cetron, M., and O'Toole, T. *Encounters with the future: A forecast of life into the 21st century.* New York: McGraw-Hill, 1982.

This book serves as a guide for the next twenty years with data-based predictions on such topics as careers, family, investments, health, and longevity.

Cornish, E. (Ed.) *The future: A guide to information sources.* Bethesda, Md.: World Future Society, 1977.

This is a guide to individuals, organizations, educational programs, periodicals and books, films and tapes, games and simulations. Other information sources are also given.

Cornish, E. (Ed.) *1999—The world of tomorrow.* Bethesda, Md.: World Future Society, 1978.

This first anthology of articles from the journal, *The Futurist,* chronicles diverse areas of concern pertinent to the future. Forecasting, space, oceanography, future businesses, medicine, population, education, energy, technology, and recycling are among the topics discussed.

Dickson, P. *The future file: A guide for people with one foot in the 21st century.* Bethesda, Md.: World Future Society, 1977.

A general overview of futurism and future studies is the central focus of this work. An almanac and futures directory are included.

Eggers, J. *Will you help me create the future?* Buffalo, N.Y.: Disseminators of Knowledge, Publishers, 1981.

Forty-five futuristic student activities are presented in language arts, social studies, mathematics, and science.

Hollister, B., and Thompson, D. *Grokking the future: Science fiction in the classroom.* Fairfield, N.J.: Pflaum-Standard, 1973.

Suggestions are presented for teachers who are utilizing science fiction to assist their students in studying the future. Ideas are given for science fiction readings, exercises, and questions. Topics include ecology, social order, future cities, machines, atomic weapons, and economic trends.

Kauffman, D. *Futurism and future studies: Development in classroom instruction.* Washington, D.C.: National Education Association, 1976.

Suggestions are offered for incorporating future studies in the classroom. Teaching methods include the alternative future approach; systems, stability, and change; social, economic, and political issues; and psychology of the future.

Kauffman, D. *Teaching the future: A guide to future-oriented education.* Palm Springs, Calif.: ETC Publications, 1976.

Teaching methods and resources for teaching the future are the central focus of this publication. Exercises on ways of thinking about the future are suggested. The activities are applicable to a variety of ages.

Toffler, A. *Future shock.* New York: Random House, 1970.

The author provides a thorough documentation and description of the increasing impact of change upon our society and upon the individual. The importance of preparing for the future in a rapidly and radically changing world is stressed.

Toffler, A. (Ed.) *The futurists.* Random House, 1972.

A compilation of articles on the future and the problems of the future by leading social critics, scientists, philosophers, and planners is provided. A bibliography completes this work.

Toffler, A. (Ed.) *Learning for tomorrow—The role of the future in education.* New York: Random House, 1974.

Leaders in the field of futurism address the place of the future in the curriculum and the implementation of tomorrow's curriculum today. Specific treatment is given to values, science, and humanities in future-oriented education. A directory of institutions incorporating futuristic courses in the curriculum is provided.

GROUP DYNAMICS

Gazda, G., et al. *Human relations development: A manual for educators,* 2nd ed. Newton, Mass.: Allyn and Bacon, 1977.

A guide to the development in listening and communicating for teachers and prospective teachers is given. A rationale for human relations training and a system for its development are presented.

Hyman, R. *Improving discussion leadership.* New York: Teachers College Press, 1980.

Topics discussed are: planning a discussion, discussion skills, preventing and solving discussion problems, discussion feedback and evaluation, and improving discussion leadership. In addition, a minicourse in logic is provided for the discussion leader.

Johnson, D., and Johnson, F. *Joining together: Group theory and group skills.* Englewood Cliffs, N.J.: Prentice-Hall, 1975.

Provided in this book are the theory and experiences to develop an understanding of group dynamics.

Miles, M. *Learning to work in groups: A practical guide for members and trainers,* 2nd ed. New York: Teachers College Press, 1981.

This book contains ideas for planning training sessions, including types of training activities, the role of the trainer, and the evaluation process.

Schmuck, R., and Schmuck, P. *Group processes in the classroom.* Dubuque, Iowa: Wm. C. Brown Group, 1971.

Group dynamics theory in education is explained initially. Group processes are examined in terms of influences, communication, leadership, developmental stages, cohesiveness, norms, attractions, and organizational characteristics.

Stanford, G., and Stanford, B. *Learning discussion skills through games.* Englewood Cliffs, N.J.: Citation Press, 1969.

Specific techniques of discussion, debate, and group dynamics are illustrated with suggested activities. Methods for organization, listening, responding, and contributing are offered.

LEADERSHIP

Burns, J.M. *Leadership*. New York: Harper & Row, 1978.

In this Pulitzer prize winning book, the relationship between leadership and followship is discussed. The concepts of transactional and transforming leadership as well as moral leadership are detailed.

Flores, E.Y. *Teaching your child to lead: A parent's guide*. Palo Alto, Calif.: R & E Research Associates, 1982.

This guide is directed toward providing parents with the knowledge and the insights to assist their children to become leaders. Topics such as developing a positive leadership image, characteristics of successful leaders, and tasks of administrative leadership are discussed.

Gallagher, J. *Leadership unit*. New York: Trillium Press, 1982.

Designed for use with fifth and sixth grade gifted students, the unit contains suggestions for the study of leadership through a variety of activities. Forms and references are provided.

Gordon, T. *Leadership effectiveness training*. Ridgefield, Conn.: Wyden Books, 1977.

Ways to become a more effective leader are discussed, including listening skills, planning evaluation conferences, and methods to assist others in solving their own problems.

McCall, M., and Lombardo, M. *Leadership: Where else can we go?* Durham, N.C.: Duke University Press, 1978.

This compilation of essays, originally presented at a conference sponsored by the Center for Creative Leadership, centers on the current status in research of leadership development and training. Future research needs are stated.

Magoon, R., and Jellen, H. *Leadership development: Democracy in action*. Poquoson, Va.: Human Development Press, 1980.

This book contains twenty-four strategies for the development of leadership with the school. Forms, scales, and checklists are provided.

Stodgill, R.M. *Handbook of leadership: A survey of theory and research.* New York: Free Press, 1974.

The concepts on leadership described include definitions, theories, functions, behavior, and emergence of the leadership role. Leadership-follower interactions and leadership and group performance are discussed.

MATH AND SCIENCE

Carin, A., and Sand, R. *Teaching science through discovery.* Columbus, Ohio: Charles E. Merrill, Publishing, 1970.

The discovery-oriented elementary science curriculum is discussed. Sample discovery lesson plans are presented in ecology, evolution, electricity, light, astronomy, meteorology, anatomy, and physiology.

DeVito, A., and Krockover, G. *Creative sciencing I, A practical approach.* Boston: Little, Brown, 1976.

Useful strategies to individualize instruction in various content areas through the utilization of interest centers, task cards, and modules are contained in this book. Ideas span primary, intermediate, and middle school curricular activities.

DeVito, A., and Krockover, G. *Creative sciencing II, Ideas and activities for teachers and children.* Boston: Little, Brown, 1976.

Numerous activities to stimulate science skills in a variety of subject areas are illustrated. Science skills include classification, inferring, prediction, data interpretation, and building models. Science areas included are biology, chemistry, earth science, environmental science, and physics.

Fox, L., Brody, L., and Tobin, D. (Eds.) *Women and the mathematical mystique.* Baltimore, Md.: Johns Hopkins University Press, 1980.
The focus of this publication is the sex differences in mathematical ability. Research is reported and possible causes for the differences are discussed.

McGavack, J., and LaSalle, D. *Crystals, insects, and unknown objects: A creative approach to the teaching of science to intermediate school children.* Scranton, Pa.: John Day, 1971.

This book is a continuation of the philosophy and practical activities of the authors with emphasis on the intermediate level. The focus is upon total student involvement in the scientific process.

McGavack, J., and LaSalle, D. *Guppies, bubbles and vibrating objects.* Scranton, Pa.: John Day, 1969.

Suggested activities in science for early childhood students are enumerated. Pictorial illustrations accompany most of the activities. Bibliographies of reading materials and films with accompanying lists of publishers and addresses are included.

Piltz, A., and Sund, R. *Creative teaching of science in the elementary school,* 2nd ed. Newton, Mass.: Allyn and Bacon, 1974.

The author sets forth a variety of activities for incorporating creativity into the teaching of science. Emphasis is upon student involvement and active participation in scientific learning.

Stanley, J., et al. (Eds.) *Mathematical talent, discovery, description, and development* (Hyman Blumberg Symposium on Research in Early Childhood Education) Baltimore, Md.: Johns Hopkins University Press, 1974.

A report focusing on mathematically and scientifically precocious youth based on a five-year study at Johns Hopkins University and the results of various concomitant research studies is set forth.

Suchman, J. *Inquiry development program in earth science.* New York: Trillium Press, 1981.

Ideas for observations and conducting experiments in earth science are given.

Westcott, A., and Smith, J. *Creative teaching of mathematics in the elementary school,* 2nd ed. Newton, Mass.: Allyn and Bacon, 1978.

Techniques for the creative teaching of language arts, reading, social studies, mathematics, and science are found in this book. Illustrations enhance the usefulness of the suggestions.

READING AND LANGUAGE ARTS

Cushenbery, D., and Howell, H. *Reading and the gifted child: A guide for teachers.* Springfield, Ill.: Charles C. Thomas, Publisher, 1974.

A guide to activities for stimulating and extending language arts and reading with gifted students at elementary and secondary levels is given. Reading materials appropriate for the gifted are listed.

Kenny, A. *A creative writing companion.* Woodcliff Lake, N.J.: New Dimensions for the 80's Publishers, 1981.

Activities in this book are written to enhance the writing skills of students studying topics in *The Investigation of Real Problems.* Ways to assist students to publish are presented.

Knight, L. *Language arts for the exceptional: The gifted and linguistically different.* Itasca, Ill.: F.E. Peacock, Publishers, 1974.

The unique needs of gifted students are addressed through specific activities for improving skills in listening and communication, oral and written.

Labuda, M. (Ed.) *Creative reading for gifted learners: A design for excellence.* Newark, Del.: International Reading Association, 1974.

This compilation of readings focuses on the nature and needs of gifted students at the elementary and secondary levels in reading, creativity, and language arts. Many activities for challenging the gifted student in the area of reading are suggested.

Liatsos, S. *Reading comprehension: A springboard to creative thinking.* Buffalo, N.Y.: Disseminators of Knowledge, Publishers, 1977.

Guilford's analysis of creative thinking is employed to determine activities in reading comprehension. Detailed activities and descriptions contribute to the usefulness of this resource for teachers.

Pilon, B. *Teaching language arts creatively in the elementary grades.* New York: John Wiley and Sons, 1978.

A practical guide for elementary teachers to enhance the creative abilities of students through innovation in language arts is provided. Suggestions for writing, literature, spelling, and reading are given.

Smith, J. *Creative teaching of language arts in the elementary school,* 2nd ed. Newton, Mass.: Allyn and Bacon, 1973.

Many practical suggestions are described utilizing creative teaching in listening, oral expression, creative writing, handwriting, and spelling.

Smith, J. *Creative teaching of reading and literature in elementary schools.* Newton, Mass.: Allyn and Bacon, 1967.

A practical approach for the teaching of reading, literature, and poetry is discussed for the regular classroom teacher at the primary and intermediate levels. Suggestions for developing creativity in children through these areas are discussed.

Smith, J. *Creative teaching of reading in the elementary school,* 2nd ed. Newton, Mass.: Allyn and Bacon, 1975.

Additional topics provided in this edition include the open school philosophy, linguistics, and behavioral objectives. Practical suggestions for all aspects of reading are provided for pre-service and in-service teachers.

Warren, B. *Capture creativity: Photographs to inspire young writers.* Tucson, Ariz.: Communication Skill Builders, 1983.

This book combines English and creativity with the elements of photography. Many photographs are incorporated.

Witty, P. (Ed.) *Reading for the gifted and creative student.* Newark, Del.: International Reading Association, 1971.

Suggestions are provided for appropriate instruction and experiences in reading programs for the gifted and creative. Innovative educational programs are cited, as well as the roles of the family and the teacher in effectuating reading.

SOCIAL STUDIES

Bucher, C. *Activities for today's social studies.* Dansville, N.Y.: Instructor Publications, 1973.

This handbook provides teaching suggestions and practical activities for younger students in a variety of social science areas. Learning activities in social processes, human relations, cultures, and current affairs are included. General social science skills are incorporated, as well as the fields of anthropology, sociology, history, economics, geography, and political science.

Crosby, N., and Marten, N. *Discovering psychology.* Buffalo, N.Y.: Disseminators of Knowledge, Publishers, 1981.

The activities in this book focus on affective development. Personal, social, and emotional adjustment is emphasized.

Hennessey, G. *Discovering economics.* Buffalo, N.Y.: Disseminators of Knowledge, Publishers, 1981.

Among the economic concepts developed in this book are inflation, taxes, banks, gross national product, and supply and demand.

McCarthy, G., and Marso, M. *Discovering archaeology.* Buffalo, N.Y.: Disseminators of Knowledge, Publishers, 1981.

Previous cultures are studied through the activities presented. Related activities are also suggested.

Smith, J. *Creative teaching of social studies in the elementary school,* 2nd ed. Newton, Mass.: Allyn and Bacon, 1978.

Creative teaching practices in social living, including values and character development, study skills, and the use of audiovisual materials are described and illustrated for the elementary teacher.

Youngers, J., and Aceti, J. *Simulation games and activities for social studies.* Danville, N.Y.: Instructor Publications, 1974.

Teachers of younger students may find numerous simulation suggestions which may be implemented in the social science component of the curriculum. Guidelines for simulations on economics, ranging from bartering to competition and profit, are included.

VALUES CLARIFICATION

Ballard, J. *A leader handbook for conducting circletime: A curriculum of affect.* New York: Irvington, Publishers, 1982.

Contained in this handbook is a listing of awareness activities in the affective domain. A reference list of books on the topic is included.

Casteel, J., and Stahl, R. *Value clarification in the classroom: A primer.* Santa Monica, Calif.: Goodyear Publishing, 1975.

This book is intended to aid teachers in the organization and guidance of instruction in values clarification. Sample value clarification sheets are provided in the areas of social studies, human relations, feminism, and career education.

Castillo, G. *Left-handed teaching: Lessons in affective education.* New York: Holt, Rinehart and Winston, 1978.

Practical suggestions for integrating cognitive and affective teaching in the classroom are given. Model units are presented for practical implementation in the classroom.

Curwin, R., et al. *Developing individual values in the classroom.* Palo Alto, Calif.: Learning Handbooks, 1974.

Values clarification strategies are explained with examples of discussion questions to follow the activities. Integration of values into language arts, social studies, science, and mathematics is illustrated. Suggestions are given for the creation of new values clarification activities, and an annotated bibliography is provided.

Eberle, R., and Hall, R. *Affective direction: Planning and teaching for thinking and feeling.* Buffalo, N.Y.: Disseminators of Knowledge, Publishers, 1979.

This guide to affective education contains models, teaching strategies, and suggested materials. Information on lesson plans and topics to enhance affectivity are included.

Eberle, R., and Hall, R. *Affective education guidebook.* Buffalo, N.Y.: Disseminators of Knowledge, Publishers, 1975.

A guide for the teacher interested in the development of feelings in students is given with over one hundred activities to assist the student in understanding and expressing feelings. Suggestions are given for group discussions and problem solving techniques.

Elder, C. *Making value judgments: Decisions for today.* Columbus, Ohio: Charles E. Merrill, Publishing, 1972.

The nature of values and techniques of making values decisions are set forth. Various activities incorporating important issues and situations involving values decisions which have been encountered by famous people are provided for the intermediate and junior high school teacher.

Galbraith, R., and Jones, T. *Moral reasoning: A teaching handbook for adapting Kohlberg to the classroom.* St. Paul, Minn.: Greenhaven Press, 1976.

Kohlberg's six-stage theory of moral reasoning is explained. The teaching process and methods of teaching for moral development are provided. Suggested moral dilemmas for classroom implementation are also contained in this volume.

Hall, R. *Moral education: A handbook for teachers.* Minneapolis, Minn.: Winston Press, 1979.

Developed through the Moral Education Project, this book describes five strategies for teaching moral development. Teaching units in social studies, economics, humanities, behavioral sciences, and personal relations are included.

Harmin, M., Kirschenbaum, H., and Simon, S. *Clarifying values through subject matter: Applications for the classroom.* Minneapolis, Minn.: Winston Press, 1973.

This additional manuscript of the authors' combines previous writings in the area of values clarification and subject matter in the curriculum. The three-level strategy for teaching subject matter is discussed, and suggestions are provided for the implementation of values clarification in all areas of the curriculum.

Hawley, R. *Values exploration through role playing.* New York: Hart, Publishing, 1975.

Diverse techniques for utilizing role-playing strategies to develop values clarification in the classroom are discussed. Subject matter is integrated with values clarification. The relationship of role playing to moral development is explained.

Hawley, R., Simon, S., and Britton, D. *Composition for personal growth: Values clarification through writing.* New York: Hart, Publishing, 1973.

This is primarily a program to teach writing composition with an emphasis on values clarification. Many original activities are presented.

Hersh, R., Paolitto, D., and Reimer, J. *Promoting moral growth from Piaget to Kohlberg.* New York: Longman, 1979.

The philosophical and psychological foundations of the two theories are explained. School-related examples are given for the teacher to turn theory into practice.

Kirschenbaum, H. *Clarifying values clarification: Some theoretical issues.* Saratoga, New York: National Humanistic Education Center, 1975.

The author explains his personal concept of the valuing process which includes the dimensions of thinking, feeling, choosing, communicating, and acting.

Kirschenbaum, H. *Advanced values clarification: A handbook for teachers, counselors and experienced teachers.* Saratoga, New York: National Humanistic Education Center, 1976.

The most recent book on values clarification incorporates theories and research, designing values experiences, and building values into the curriculum. An annotated bibliography spanning 1965–75 completes the text.

Kniker, C. *You and values education.* Columbus, Ohio: Charles E. Merrill, Publishing, 1977.

Educators are given an introduction to values education. Suggestions for the adoption of particular approaches to values instruction are an integral part of the book. Emphasis is upon choosing values education strategies that work most effectively for the individual. Nine approaches to values education are incorporated.

Mattox, B. *Getting it together: Dilemmas for the classroom.* San Diego, Calif.: Pennant Press, 1975.

The author intends this book to serve as a starting point for working with Kohlberg's moral development approach to values education. Outlined are Kohlberg's approach, stages of moral development, and various teaching techniques to implement values education in the classroom.

Piaget, J. *Moral judgment of the child.* New York: P.F. Collier, 1962.

An overview of Piaget's developmental theory of morality in children includes the following four states: pre-moral, obedience to adult authority, autonomous-reciprocity, and autonomous-ideal reciprocity.

Presno, V., and Presno, C. *The values realm.* New York: Teachers College Press, 1980.

Suggestions for teachers to develop activities in values clarification are given in the following areas: psychological, social, economic, ethical, esthetic, poetic and literary, technology, and legal.

Raths, L., Harmin, M., and Simon, S. *Values and teaching: Working with values in the classroom.* Columbus, Ohio: Charles E. Merrill, Publishing, 1966.

This first major work on values clarification combines theory and practical classroom approaches. The theoretical section focuses upon the difficulty of developing values and teaching for values clarity. Activities for the classroom teacher incorporate guidelines, problems, and procedures for initiating values clarification.

Read, D., and Simon, S. *Humanistic education sourcebook.* Englewood Cliffs, N.J.: Prentice-Hall, 1975.

This book of readings deals with the implementation of humanistic education theory in the classroom. Activities for classroom use to develop awareness of self and others are contained in several of the articles.

Ringness, T. *The affective domain in education.* Boston: Little, Brown, 1975.

An overview of the affective domain with both the behaviorist and humanist view is presented. This book was written as an overview for education majors.

Rucker, W., Amspiger, V., and Brodbeck, A. *Human values in the classroom.* Dubuque, Iowa: Kendall/Hunt Publishing, 1969.

This book is the original teachers' guide for the utilization of the

Lasswell-Ruckers values framework. This framework is explained and suggested classroom practices are enumerated.

Scharf, P., McCoy, W., and Ross, D. *Growing up moral: Dilemmas for the intermediate grades.* Minneapolis, Minn.: Winston Press, 1979.

The theory of preadolescent moral growth is presented and over fifty exercises in moral development are included.

Shaftel, F., and Shaftel, G. *Role-playing for social values: Decision-making in social studies.* Englewood Cliffs, N.J.: Prentice-Hall, 1967.

The first section of the book deals with role playing and its implementation. The second section presents a series of problem situations which may be adapted for role playing.

Simon, S., and Clark, J. *Beginning values clarification: Strategies for the classroom.* San Diego, Calif.: Pennant Press, 1975.

The rationale for values clarification is explained; guidelines for working with groups on values clarification activities are outlined; and specific strategies and activities for values clarification on diverse topics are presented.

Simon, S., Howe, L., and Kirschenbaum, H. *Values clarification: A handbook of practical strategies for teachers and students.* New York: Hart Publishing, 1972.

The second major work on values clarification describes seventy-nine values activities for the classroom. Methods, rationale, examples, and teacher explanations are provided with each strategy. Examples are grouped according to various age levels.

Simpson, B. *Becoming aware of values.* San Diego, Calif.: Pennant, Press, 1973.

This book, which is based upon the Lasswell-Rucker values framework, is divided into three sections. Section 1 discusses the concept of values and its purposes, procedures, and processes. Section 2 describes materials and activities for values education. Section 3 provides additional background information for teachers.

Superka, D., et al. *Values education sourcebook: Conceptual approaches, materials, analyses, and an annotated bibliography.* San Diego, Calif.: Pennant, Press, 1976.

The authors present a classification scheme for various approaches to values education, an instrument for evaluating values education materials, and an annotated bibliography of resources in values education.

Valett, R. *Affective—Humanistic education.* Belmont, Calif.: Pitman, Learning, 1974.

Affective learning goals and objectives are established. A program rationale and a program guide for affective education are detailed. This volume also contains a variety of activities and commercial materials.

Valett, R. *Humanistic education—Developing the total person.* St. Louis, Mo.: C.V. Mosby, 1977.

The author defines humanistic education and establishes affective-humanistic objectives. Curriculum guides, pilot studies, and commercial models are described and referenced.

RELATED TOPICS

Blake, J., and Ernst, B. *The great perpetual learning machine.* Boston: Little, Brown, 1976.

Numerous learning activities for children in the sciences, language arts, music, art, math, logic, and probability are described. Many illustrations are included with the practical suggestions. Bibliographies of various teaching materials, books, references, and resources are provided.

Bloom, B. (Ed.) *Taxonomy of educational objectives, handbook 1: Cognitive domain.* New York: David McKay, 1956.

A hierarchical classification system of cognitive processes is delineated and described. Specific questions and suggestions for teaching methods are set forth for each level.

Cardoza, P., and Menten, T. *The whole kids' catalog.* New York: Bantam Books, 1975.

A potpourri of ideas and activities having wide appeal is presented. Topics include magic, photography, ecology, sports, science, space, films, and yoga. References for obtaining free and inexpensive materials are given.

Eggen, P.D., Kauchak, D.P., and Harder, R.J. *Strategies for teachers: Information processing models in the classroom.* Englewood Cliffs, N.J.: Prentice-Hall, 1979.

Described in this book are six information processing models and ways they can be employed with a variety of students in various learning situations.

Fingeroth, M., and Fingeroth, P. *Miniguides: Sixteen ready-made minicourses.* Englewood Cliffs, N.J.: Citation Press, 1975.

This is a compilation of sixteen diverse minicourses prepared by experienced teachers. Suggestions are offered for a variety of activities in several areas of endeavor. Topics covered in these minicourses for junior high students are humor, peace, survival, mysteries, American labor, death, and science fiction.

Furth, H., and Wacks, H. *Thinking goes to school: Piaget's theory in practice.* New York: Oxford University Press, 1974.

Educators are provided a usable guide to Piagetian theory with suggestions of thinking activities based upon Piagetian stages of cognitive development. One hundred seventy-nine games and exercises for primary age children are included.

Goodson, D. *How to start an interschool quiz competition.* Goleta, California: University Research Company, 1977.

Procedures for developing and implementing quiz competition programs for students are given. Suggestions are provided for teachers and administrators.

Guilford, J. *The nature of human intelligence.* New York: McGraw-Hill, 1967.

This is a comprehensive explanation of the structure of intellectual processes, including 120 postulated intellectual abilities.

Guilford, J. *Way beyond the I.Q.* Buffalo, N.Y.: Creative Education

Foundation, and Great Neck, N.Y.: Creative Synergetic Associates, 1977.

Intelligence is examined as a multifaceted construct, composed of 150 distinct abilities. Chapters are devoted to the various kinds of information, products, and operations. Activities, specific examples, and tests for the development of these mental operations are presented.

Karlin, M. *Classroom activities deskbook for fun and learning.* Englewood Cliffs, N.J.: Prentice-Hall, 1975.

The purpose of this book is to provide the regular classroom teacher with suggested activities and resources for teaching to students of all levels of ability. Although not all of the activities would be appropriate for gifted students, teachers may find several activities for use with their gifted students.

Kratwohl, D., et al. Taxonomy of educational objectives, the classification of educational goals, handbook II: Affective domain. New York: David McKay, 1964.

A hierarchical classification of the affective domain is presented and explained. Activities for the development of values are set forth.

Levin, J., and Allen, V. *Cognitive learning in children: Theories and strategies.* New York: Academic Press, 1976.

This book deals with the presumed cognitive abilities of children in various learning situations. The instructional training techniques that facilitate the learning process are outlined. In addition, concrete examples on the improvement of classroom instruction are provided.

Massialas, B., and Zevin, J. *Creative encounters in the classroom: Teaching and learning through discovery.* New York: John Wiley and Sons, 1967.

The inquiry approach, analytical thinking, creative thinking, and values examination are discussed. Teaching strategies based upon discovery and inquiry methods are proposed. Training students as investigators is advocated.

Meeker, M. *The structure of intellect: Its interpretation and uses.* Columbus, Ohio: Charles E. Merrill, Publishing, 1969.

Guilford's Structure of the Intellect model is explained in detail and translated into educational activities focusing on the various abilities subsumed in the model.

Oliver, A. *Maximizing minicourses: A practical guide to a curriculum alternative.* New York: Teachers College Press, 1978.

Details of purpose and underlying assumptions of minicourses are presented. Ideas and suggestions for all subjects at the elementary and secondary levels are offered for classroom teachers and curriculum specialists.

Provenzo, A., and Provenzo, E. *Play it again.* Englewood Cliffs, N.J.: Prentice-Hall, 1981.

The focus of this book is historic board games which can be made and played. Information on rules of gamemanship, useful strategies, tools and supplies, and suggestions for making playing pieces are some of the areas covered.

Shulman, L., and Keislar, E. *Learning by discovery: A critical appraisal.* Skokie, Ill.: Rand McNally, 1966.

Based upon conference proceedings at a conference on Learning by Discovery at Stanford University, various authors, including Bruner, Kagan, Glaser, and Gagne, discuss and analyze the discovery method of learning.

Williams, F. *Classroom ideas for encouraging thinking and feeling.* Buffalo, N.Y.: Disseminators of Knowledge, Publishers, 1970.

Williams' model of cognitive and affective interaction is the basis for suggestions for teaching methodologies to stimulate productive thinking.

Worthy, M. *A puzzle approach to creative thinking.* Chicago: Nelson-Hall, Publishers, 1975.

A variety of puzzlers are provided: embedded words, flexibility, anagrams, lost letters, and regroup puzzles. Solutions require creative thinking and alternative mind-sets.

Wurman, R. (Ed.) *Yellow pages of learning resources.* Cambridge, Mass.: MIT Press, 1972.

This is a practical guide of suggestions for utilizing community resources in the curriculum, incorporating the format of the yellow pages of the telephone directory. The child may discover ideas for independent study and projects.

PUBLISHERS AND ADDRESSES

Academic Press, Inc.
111 5th Avenue
New York, NY 10003

Adapt Press, Inc.
1209 West Bailey
Sioux Falls, SD 57104

**Addison-Wesley Publishing
Co., Inc.**
Reading, MA 01867

Aldine Publishing Co.
200 Saw Mill River Road
Hawthorne, NY 10532

Allan Associates, Inc.
Starkville, MS 29759

Allyn and Bacon, Inc.
7 Wells Avenue
Newton, MA 02159

Aspen Systems Corp.
1600 Research Boulevard
Rockville, MD 20850

Ayer Co.
99 Main Street
Salem, NH 03079

Badger Press
P.O. Box 25
Cross Plains, WI 53528

Bantam Books, Inc.
666 5th Avenue
New York, NY 10103

A.S. Barnes and Co., Inc.
11175 Flintkote Avenue
San Diego, CA 92121

Basic Books, Inc., Publishers
10 East 53rd Street
New York, NY 10022

Beacon Press
25 Beacon Street
Boston, MA 02108

**Berkshire Community Press,
Inc.**
P.O. Box 1312
Pittsfield, MA 01202

R.R. Bowker Co.
1180 Avenue of the Americas
New York, NY 10036

Wm. C. Brown Group
2460 Kerper Boulevard
Dubuque, IA 52001

Center for Creative Learning
P.O. Box 85
Williamsville, NY 14221

Christopher Publishing House
1405 Hanover Street
West Hanover, MA 02339

**Communication Skill Builders,
Inc.**
3130 N. Dodge Boulevard
P.O. Box 42050
Tucson, AZ 85733

Copp Clark Pitman
517 Wellington Street W
Toronto, Ontario, M5V 1G1

Council for Exceptional
  Children
1920 Association Drive
Reston, VA 22091

Crane, Russak and Co., Inc.
3 East 44th Street
New York, NY 10017

Creative Computing Press
P.O. Box 789-M
Morristown, NJ 07960

Creative Learning Press
P.O. Box 320
Mansfield Center, CT 06250

Creative Publications
P.O. Box 10328
Palo Alto, CA 94303

Creative Synergetic Associates,
  Ltd.
4623-26 1st Street
Great Neck, NY 11020

Croft-NEI Publications
24 Rope Ferry Road
Waterford, CT 06386

John Day Co., Inc.
Harper & Row Publications
Scranton, PA 18512

Disseminators of Knowledge,
  Publishers
71 Radcliffe Road
Buffalo, NY 14214

Doubleday and Co., Inc.
Garden City, NY 11530

Duke University Press
6697 College Station
Durham, NC 27708

E.P. Dutton, Inc.
2 Park Avenue
New York, NY 10016

EDITS Publishers
P.O. Box 7234
San Diego, CA 92107

ERIC Clearinghouse on Teach-
  er Education
One Dupont Circle
Washington, D.C. 20005

ETC Publications
P.O. Drawer 1627-A
Palm Springs, CA 92262

Foundation for Exceptional
  Children
1920 Association Drive
Reston, VA 22091

The Free Press
866 3rd Avenue
New York, NY 10022

Goodyear Publishing Co.
6040 5th Street
Santa Monica, CA 90401

Greenhaven Press, Inc.
577 Shoreview Park Road
St. Paul, MN 55112

Greenwood Press
88 Post Road West
P.O. Box 5007
Westport, CT 06881

Grune and Stratton, Inc.
111 5th Avenue
New York, NY 10003

Halsted Press
605 3rd Avenue
New York, NY 10158

Harper & Row Ltd.
28 Tavestock Street
London WC2E 7PN

Harper & Row Publishers, Inc.
10 East 53rd Street
New York, NY 10022

Harvard University Press
79 Garden Street
Cambridge, MA 02138

D.C. Heath and Co.
125 Spring Street
Lexington, MA 02173

Holt, Rinehart and Winston General Book
521 5th Avenue
New York, NY 10175

Houghton Mifflin Company
One Beacon Street
Boston, MA 02107

Human Development Press, Ltd.
Box 2277
Poquoson, VA 23662

Humanities Press, Inc.
171 1st Avenue
Atlantic Highlands, NJ 07716

Indiana University Press
Tenth and Morton Streets
Bloomington, IN 47401

The Instructor Publications, Inc.
Dansville, NY 14437

International Reading Association
800 Barksdale Road
Newark, DE 19711

The Interstate Printers and Publishers, Inc.
19 N. Jackson Street
P.O. Box 594
Danville, IL 61832

Irvington Publishers, Inc.
551 Fifth Avenue
New York, NY 10176

Johns Hopkins University Press
Baltimore, MD 21218

Jossey-Bass, Inc., Publishers
433 California Street
San Francisco, CA 94104

Kendall/Hunt Publishing Co.
2460 Kerper Boulevard
Dubuque, IA 52001

Alfred A. Knopf, Inc.
201 East 50th Street
New York, NY 10022

Kollek and Son, Ltd.
6 Hazanovitch Street
Jerusalem, Israel

R.E. Krieger Publishing Co., Inc.
P.O. Box 9542
Melbourne, FL 32901

Learning Handbooks
530 University Avenue
Palo Alto, CA 94301

Libraries Unlimited, Inc.
P.O. Box 263
Littleton, CO 80160-0263

Little, Brown and Co.
34 Beacon Street
Boston, MA 02106

Longman, Inc.
19 West 44th Street
New York, NY 10036

Macmillan Publishing Co., Inc.
866 3rd Avenue
New York, NY 10022

McGraw-Hill Book Co.
1221 Avenue of the Americas
New York, NY 10020

David McKay Co., Inc.
2 Park Avenue
New York, NY 10016

Mafex Associates, Inc.
90 Cherry Street, Box 519
Johnstown, PA 15902

Charles E. Merrill Publishing
Co.
1300 Alum Creek Drive
Columbus, OH 43216

The MIT Press
28 Carleton Street
Cambridge, MA 02142

Monarch Press
1230 Avenue of the Americas
New York, NY 10020

C.V. Mosby Co.
11830 Westline Industrial Drive
St. Louis, MO 63141

Multi Media Arts
Box 14486
Austin, TX 78761

National Association of State
Boards of Education
526 Hall of the States
444 North Capital Street, NW
Washington, D.C. 20001

National Education Association
1201 16th Street, N.W.
Washington, D.C. 20036

National Humanistic Education
Center
111 Spring Street
Saratoga, NY 12866

National School of Public
Relations Association
1801 N. Moore Street
Arlington, VA 22209

The National Society for the
Study of Education
5835 Kimbark Avenue
Chicago, IL 60637

National/State Leadership
Training Institute on the
Gifted and Talented
Ventura County Superintendent
of Schools
535 East Main Street
Ventura, CA 93009

Nelson-Hall Publishers
111 North Canal Street
Chicago, IL 60606

The New American Library, Inc.
1633 Broadway
New York, NY 10019

**New Dimensions for the 80's
  Publishers**
P.O. Box 8559
Woodcliff Lake, NJ 07675

**Ohio Psychology Publishing
  Company**
5 East Long Street, Suite 610
Columbus, OH 43215

Olympus Publishing Co.
1670 E. 13th Street S.
Salt Lake City, UT 84105

The Oryx Press
2214 North Central at Encanto
Phoenix, AZ 85004

Oxford University Press, Inc.
200 Madison Avenue
New York, NY 10016

Parker Publishing Co., Inc.
P.O. Box 500
Englewood Cliffs, NJ 07632

F.E. Peacock Publishers, Inc.
115 North Prospect Avenue
Itasca, IL 60143

Penguin Books
625 Madison Avenue
New York, NY 10022

Pennant Press
7620 Miramer Road
San Diego, CA 92126

Pflaum-Standard
c/o CEBCO Standard
  Publishing
9 Kulick Road
Fairfield, NJ 07006

Phi Delta Kappa, Inc.
8th and Union
P.O. Box 789
Bloomington, IN 47402

Pitman Learning, Inc.
6 Davis Drive
Belmont, CA 94002

Prentice-Hall, Inc.
Englewood Cliffs, NJ 07632

Prologue Publications
P.O. Box 640
Menlo Park, CA 94025

The Putnam Publishing Group
200 Madison Avenue
New York, NY 10016

R & E Research Associates, Inc.
936 Industrial Avenue
Palo Alto, CA 94303

Rand McNally and Co.
8255 Central Park Avenue
Skokie, IL 60076

Random House, Inc.
201 East 50th Street
New York, NY 10022

Richards Rosen Press, Inc.
29 East 21st Street
New York, NY 10010

Ronald Press Co.
605 3rd Avenue
New York, NY 10058

Routledge and Kegan Paul of
     America, Ltd.
9 Park Street
Boston, MA 02108

Scarecrow Press, Inc.
52 Liberty Street
P.O. Box 656
Metuchen, NJ 08840

Schocken Books, Inc.
200 Madison Avenue
New York, NY 10016

Scholastic Book Services
50 West 44th Street
New York, NY 10036

Science Research Associates,
     Inc.
155 North Wacker Drive
Chicago, IL 60606

Scott, Foresman and Co.
1900 East Lake Avenue
Glenview, IL 60025

The Scribner Book
     Companies, Inc.
597 Fifth Avenue
New York, NY 10017

The Shoe String Press, Inc.
995 Sherman Avenue
P.O. Box 4327
Hamden, CT 06514

Special Learning Corp.
42 Boston Post Road
Guilford, CT 06437

Stanford University Press
Stanford, CA 94305

Sterling Swift Publishing Co.
1600 Fortview Road
Austin, TX 78704

Teachers College Press
Columbia University
1234 Amsterdam Avenue
New York, NY 10027

Teaching Resources Corp.
50 Pond Park Road
Hingham, MA 02043

Charles C Thomas, Publisher
2600 South 1st Street
Springfield, IL 62717

Trillium Press
P.O. Box 921, Madison Square
     Station
New York, NY 10159

United States Government
     Printing Office
Public Documents Department
Washington, D.C. 20402

University Associates, Inc.
8517 Production Avenue
P.O. Box 26240
San Diego, CA 92126

University of Chicago Press
5801 Ellis Avenue
Chicago, IL 60637

University of Minnesota Press
2037 University Avenue, S.E.
Minneapolis, MN 55414

University Park Press
300 North Charles
Baltimore, MD 21201

University Research Co.
7581 Palos Verdes Drive
Goleta, CA 93017

**Van Nostrand Reinhold Co.,
Inc.**
135 West 50th Street
New York, NY 10020

Vantage Press
516 West 34th Street
New York, NY 10001

The Viking Press
40 West 23rd Street
New York, NY 10010

Walker and Co.
720 5th Avenue
New York, NY 10019

John Wiley and Sons, Inc.
605 3rd Avenue
New York, NY 10158

B.L. Winch and Associates
45 Hitching Post Drive,
Building 2
Rolling Hills Estates, CA 90274

Winston Press, Inc.
430 Oak Grove
Minneapolis, MN 55403

World Future Society
4916 St. Elmo Avenue
Bethesda, MD 20814

Wyden Books
P.O. Box 151
Ridgefield, CT 06877

5 Selected Games, Puzzles, and Brainteasers

The decision to include a section on games and puzzles was not made without some consternation. Our concern was that specialized education for the gifted might evolve into a curriculum consisting chiefly of games and puzzles. Since teachers and others working with gifted students often receive requests from parents for information on materials and games for their children, we decided to include them, placing emphasis on those games that are readily available. The games and puzzles selected generally may be obtained in department stores, toy shops, and bookstores. Games and puzzles were selected, not for their entertainment dimension, but for their emphasis on logical thinking and the higher cognitive processes. For the majority of games, books, and puzzles, the name and address of the company are given. However, some games and puzzles are produced by several different companies and so may be available under different trade names. Among these are chess, backgammon, three- and four-dimensional tic-tac-toe, the Tower of Hanoi Puzzle, the Fox and Geese Puzzle, and the Nine Men's Morris Puzzle. Similar games and puzzles may also be on the market. However, these particular ones have stood the test of time, both in their educational value and in their appeal to the more intelligent.

For the games listed in Table 3, the following information is given: company, name, approximate cost, design, type of game, and the general area of educational application or cognitive development. Only those games that require just a few players have been selected, since participation will more than likely take place at home. A few individual games of strategy have been included.

No suggested age range is provided since personal interests and experiences vary. Also, many of these games appeal to a wide age range. Adults as well as children often derive enjoyment from them. Prices may vary according to the place of purchase.

The games included do promote cognitive development, and parents may find that playing these games with their children is a highly effective method of expanding opportunities for learning in the home setting.

TABLE 3 GAMES

Company	Name	Cost (Approx.)	Design	Game	Educational/ Cognitive Area
Ampersand Press 691 26th Street Oakland, CA 94612	AC/DC Electric Circuits	6.00	Card	Knowledge acquisition	Science
	Krill	6.00	Card	Knowledge acquisition	Science
	Predator	5.00	Card	Knowledge acquisition	Science
	Pollination	6.00	Card	Knowledge acquisition	Science
Avalon Hill 4517 Harford Road Baltimore, MD 21214	Afrika Korps	14.00	Board	Strategy	Social Studies
	Business Strategy	14.00	Board	Strategy	Economics
	Class Struggle	16.00	Board	Strategy	Social Studies
	Diplomacy	17.00	Board	Strategy	Social Studies
	Executive Decision	14.00	Board	Strategy	Business
	Facts of Five	14.00	Board	Strategy	Memory
	Foreign Exchange	16.00	Board	Strategy	Economics
	Gettysburg	16.00	Board	Strategy	History
	Gold	22.00	Board	Strategy	Economics
	Image	16.00	Board	Strategy	Psychology
	Intern	16.00	Board	Strategy	Medicine
	Kingmaker	16.00	Board	Strategy	History
	Origins of World War II	14.00	Board	Strategy	History
	Outdoor Survival	15.00	Board	Strategy	Science
	Point of Law	16.00	Board	Strategy	Law
	1776–Game of the American Revolution	16.00	Board	Strategy	History
	Shakespeare	14.00	Board	Strategy	Literature
	The Stock Market Game	14.00	Board	Strategy	Economics
	Third Reich	16.00	Board	Strategy	History
	Tuf	17.00	Board	Strategy	Mathematics
	Tufabet	17.00	Board	Strategy	English
	Word Power	14.00	Board	Strategy	English
Cadaco, Inc. 310 West Polk Street Chicago, IL 60607	The Economy Game	7.00	Board	Strategy	Economics
	King Tut's Game	4.50	Board	Strategy	Logic
	King Tut's Game Deluxe	10.00	Board	Strategy	Logic
Creative Publications 3977 East Bayshore Road P.O. Box 10328 Palo Alto, CA 94303	Helix	8.50	Board	Strategy	Logic

TABLE 3   GAMES (continued)

Company	Name	Cost (Approx.)	Design	Game	Educational/ Cognitive Area
Creative Wargames Workshop, Inc. 330 East 6th Street Suite 1E New York, NY 10003	Junta	14.00	Board	Strategy	Economics
Fidelity Electronics, Ltd. 8800 N.W. 36th Street Miami, FL 33178	Backgammon Challenger	100.00	Board	Strategy	Logic
	Checker Challenger 2 Level	35.00	Board	Strategy	Logic
	Checker Challenger 4 Level	95.00	Board	Strategy	Logic
	Checker Challenger	115.00	Board	Strategy	Logic
	Chess Challenger	115.00	Board	Strategy	Logic
	Mini Sensory Challenger	60.00	Board	Strategy	Logic
	Reservi Challenger	155.00	Board	Strategy	Logic
Friendship Press 475 Riverside Drive New York, NY 10027	Values	6.00	Board	Role playing	Values Clarification
Ideal Toy Corp. 200 5th Avenue North New York, NY 10010	Alexander's Star	8.00	Manipulative puzzle	Strategy	Logic
	Colormatch	6.00	Card	Strategy	Logic
	Missing Link	5.00	Manipulative puzzle	Strategy	Logic
	Rubik's Cube	4.50	Manipulative puzzle	Strategy	Logic
	Rubik's Game	10.00	Manipulative puzzle	Strategy	Logic
	Rubik's Race	10.00	Manipulative puzzle	Strategy	Logic
	Rubik's Revenge	10.00	Manipulative puzzle	Strategy	Logic
	Rubik's World	10.00	Manipulative puzzle	Strategy	Logic
International Games, Inc. One Uno Circle Joliet, IL 60435	Color Cubes	9.00	Board	Strategy	Logic

TABLE 3 GAMES (continued)

Company	Name	Cost (Approx.)	Design	Game	Educational/ Cognitive Area
Kadon Enterprises, Inc. 1227 Lorene Drive, Suite 16 Pasadena, MD 21122	Leap	19.00	Board	Strategy	Logic
	Quintillions	29.00	Board	Strategy	Logic
	Proteus	27.00	Board	Strategy	Logic
	Super Quintillions	39.00	Board	Strategy	Logic
	Void	15.00	Board	Strategy	Logic
Konkuro, Inc. 1313 Laurel Street Suite 24A San Carlos, CA 94070	Konkuro	25.00	Board	Strategy	Logic
Lakeside-Cox 4400 West 78th Street Minneapolis, MN 55435	Score Four	9.00	Board	Strategy	Logic
Mag-Nif, Inc. 200 5th Avenue New York, NY 10010	Astrologic	3.50	Manipulative puzzle	Strategy	Logic
	Curious Cross	3.50	Manipulative puzzle	Strategy	Logic
	Happy Cubes	6.00	Manipulative puzzle	Strategy	Logic
	The Game of the Gods	8.50	Manipulative puzzle	Strategy	Logic
	Tri Logic	6.00	Manipulative puzzle	Strategy	Logic
	Turnabout	8.50	Board	Strategy	Logic
	Tut's Tomb	5.00	Manipulative puzzle	Strategy	Logic
	Woodn't Tri	6.00	Manipulative puzzle	Strategy	Logic
Milton Bradley Co. Springfield, MA 01101	Domination	8.00	Board	Strategy	Logic
	Electronic Stratego	43.00	Board	Strategy	Logic
	Impossi-Ball	7.00	Manipulative puzzle	Strategy	Logic
	Stratego	8.50	Board	Strategy	Logic
Parker Brothers P.O. Box 1012 Beverly, MA 01915	Big Boggle	14.00	Manipulative puzzle	Strategy	Logic
	Boggle	8.00	Manipulative puzzle	Strategy	Logic
	Clue	12.00	Board	Strategy	Logic
	Lost Treasure	11.00	Board	Strategy	Logic
	Orb	4.00	Manipulative puzzle	Strategy	Logic

TABLE 3   GAMES (continued)

Company	Name	Cost (Approx.)	Design	Game	Educational/ Cognitive Area
Parker Brothers P.O. Box 1012 Beverly, MA 01915	Pocket Boggle	8.00	Manipulative puzzle	Strategy	Logic
	Probe	12.00	Board	Word game	Language Arts
	Razzle	10.00	Board	Word game	Language Arts
	Risk	17.00	Board	Strategy	Social Studies
Pente Games, Inc. 915 S. Main Stillwater, OK 74074	Pente	17.00	Board	Strategy	Logic
Pressman Toy Co. 200 Fifth Avenue New York, NY 10001	Mastermind	8.00	Board	Strategy	Logic
	Advanced Mastermind	12.50	Board	Strategy	Logic
	Mini-Mastermind	4.00	Board	Strategy	Logic
Rex Games, Inc. 447 New Grove Street Wilkes-Barre, PA 18702	Tangoes	8.00	Board	Manipulative puzzle	Logic
Sabaki P.O. Box 23 Carlisle, PA 17013	Go	48.00	Board	Strategy	Logic
Selchow and Righter 200 5th Avenue New York, NY 10010	Changram	12.00	Board	Strategy	Logic
	Scrabble, Standard Edition	9.00	Board	Strategy	Language Arts, Logic
	Scrabble, Deluxe Edition	22.00	Board	Strategy	Language Arts, Logic
	Scrabble, Travel Edition	6.00	Board	Strategy	Language Arts, Logic
	Scrabble, Pocket Edition	4.00	Board	Strategy	Language Arts, Logic
	Quip Cubes	12.00	Board	Strategy	Language Arts, Logic
	Upper Hand	11.00	Board	Strategy	Language Arts, Logic
	Vis-a-Vis	7.00	Board	Strategy	Logic
Sleuth Publications, Ltd. 2527 24th Street San Francisco, CA 94110	Sherlock Holmes Consulting Detective Game	35.00	Board	Strategy	Logic
Southold Game Co. 12 West 90th Street Suite E New York, NY 10024	Penumbra	15.00	Board	Strategy	Logic

TABLE 3   GAMES (continued)

Company	Name	Cost (Approx.)	Design	Game	Educational/ Cognitive Area
Star Game Co. P.O. Box 1683 Manassas, VA 22110	Leverage	15.00	Board	Strategy	Logic
Systems, Inc. 380 Hospital Drive Glen Burnie, MD 21061-5783	Dataflow	15.00	Board	Strategy	Computer Science, Logic
TRS Hobbies, Inc. 722 Main Street Lake Geneva, WI 53147	Divine Right	10.00	Board	Strategy	Logic
	Dungeon	10.00	Board	Strategy	Logic
	Dungeons and Dragons, Basic Set	12.00	Board	Strategy	Logic
	Dungeons and Dragons, Expert Set	12.00	Board	Strategy	Logic
	Knights of Camelot	10.00	Board	Strategy	Logic
	Original Dungeons and Dragons, Basic Set	10.00	Board	Strategy	Logic
	War of Wizards	10.00	Board	Strategy	Logic
Ungame Co. 761 Monroe Way Placentia, CA 92670	Roll-A-Role	14.00	Board	Strategy	Values Clarification
	The Ungame	11.00	Board	Strategy	Values Clarification
WFF'N Proof Learning Games Associates 1490 South Boulevard Ann Arbor, MI 48104	Equations	13.00	Board	Strategy	Mathematics
	The Meditation Game	2.50	Board	Strategy	Logic
	On-Sets	13.00	Board	Strategy	Mathematics
	Propaganda	13.00	Board	Strategy	Language Arts, Social studies
	Queries and Theories	16.00	Board	Strategy	Logic
	Quik Sane	3.00	Puzzle	Strategy	Logic
	Tac-Tickle	2.50	Board	Strategy	Logic
	The Real Numbers Game	3.00	Board	Strategy	Mathematics
	Tri-Nim	7.00	Board	Strategy	Mathematics
	WFF	3.00	Board	Strategy	Logic
	WFF'N Proof	16.00	Board	Strategy	Logic
World Wide Games, Inc. Box 450 Delaware, OH 43015	Chinese Tangram Puzzle Puzzle	25.00	Board	Strategy	Logic
	Lucky Seven Puzzle	9.00	Board	Strategy	Logic
Xanadu Leisure, Ltd. Box 10-Q Honolulu, HA 96816	Marrakesh	50.00	Board	Strategy	Logic

BRAINTEASERS

Books of puzzles and brainteasers were also selected according to their emphasis on logical thought and the higher cognitive processes, and not on their entertainment value. However, there are numerous books of puzzles which provide enjoyment to the gifted.

The list of books of puzzles and brainteasers in Table 4 provides the following information: the name and address of the publisher, the name of the puzzle or book, and the cost of the item. Prices may vary according to place of purchase. Many of the books are available in both hardback and paperback editions.

TABLE 4   BOOKS OF BRAINTEASERS

Publisher	Name	Cost (Approx.)
Ace Books 200 Madison Avenue Box RG New York, NY 10016	Test Your Wits	$ 2.00
Addison-Wesley Publishing Co. Reading, MA 01867	The Mensa Genius Quiz Book	5.00
Banbury Books, Inc. 37 West Avenue Wayne, PA 19087	The Winning Solution The Winning Solution to Rubik's Revenge	2.50 2.50
Berkley Publishing Co. 200 Madison Avenue New York, NY 10016	More Tests and Teasers Tests and Teasers	2.50 2.50
Cambridge University Press 32 East 57th Street New York, NY 10022	Puzzle It Out	5.00
Creative Publications 3977 East Bayshore P.O. Box 10328 Palo Alto, CA 94303	The Cantebury Puzzles Puzzles Mathematical Teasers Moscow Puzzles Test Your Logic 101 Puzzles in Thought and Logic	5.50 6.00 3.50 3.50 2.00 2.00
Creative Teaching Associates 5629 East Westover P.O. Box 7766 Fresno, CA 93747	Brain Drain, Book A Brain Drain, Book B	5.00 5.00

TABLE 4   BOOKS OF BRAINTEASERS

Publisher	Name	Cost (Approx.)
Cuisenaire Co. of America, Inc. 12 Church Street, Box D New Rochelle, NY 10805	Conquer the Cube	3.00
The Dial Press 1 Dag Hammerskjold Plaza New York, NY 10017	How to Solve Rubik's Revenge	3.00
Doubleday and Co., Inc. 501 Franklin Avenue Garden City, NY 11530	Fun with Brain Puzzlers	2.00
	Games for the Superintelligent	9.00
	More Games for the Superintelligent	9.00
	Super Strategies for Puzzles and Games	11.00
Dover Publications, Inc. 180 Varick Street New York, NY 10014	Magic Squares and Cubes	5.00
	Recreations in the Theory of Numbers	5.50
	New Recreations with Magic Squares	4.00
	Magic Cubes: New Recreations	4.00
	Symbolic Logic and the Game of Logic	4.50
	Amusements in Mathematics	4.50
	Mathematical Bafflers	3.00
	Puzzles in Math and Logic	2.50
	Mathemagic	2.00
	Fun with Figures	2.00
	More Fun with Figures	2.50
	Challenging Mathematical Figures	2.50
	Mathematical Brain-Teasers	2.50
	Mathematical Diversions	2.50
	Madachy's Mathematical Recreations	3.50
	Mathematical Recreations	5.00
	Mathematical Puzzles of Sam Lloyd	2.50
	More Mathematical Puzzles of Sam Lloyd	2.50
	Mathematical Puzzles for Beginners and Enthusiasts	3.00
	My Best Puzzles in Logic and Reasoning	2.50
	The Master Book of Mathematical Recreations	5.00
	Test Your Logic	2.00
	New Puzzles in Logical Deduction	2.50
	Recreations in Logic	2.00
	101 Puzzles in Thought and Logic	2.00
	Mazes and Labyrinths: A Book of Puzzles	2.00
	Big Book of Mazes and Labyrinths	3.50
	Graphic and Op-Art Mazes	2.00

TABLE 4   BOOKS OF BRAINTEASERS

Publisher	Name	Cost (Approx.)
Dover Publications, Inc. 180 Varick Street New York, NY 10014	Mind Boggling Mazes	2.00
	Storybook Mazes	2.00
	Challenging Mazes	2.50
	The World's Most Difficult Mazes	2.50
	The 8th Book of TAN: 700 Tangrams	2.50
	Tangrams: 300 Puzzles	2.50
	The Fun with Tangrams Kit	2.00
	Tangrams ABC Kit	2.50
Emerson Books, Inc. Reynolds Lane Bachanan, NY 10511	Brain Puzzler's Delight	11.00
	Math Is Fun	10.00
	Mind Tickling Brain Teasers	10.00
	Puzzles for Pleasure	11.00
	Rubik's Cube Made Simple	2.00
	The Math Entertainer	9.00
Harper & Row, Publishers, Inc. 10 East 53rd Street New York, NY 10022	A Diversity of Puzzles	4.00
	Mathematical Carnival	5.00
	Mathematical Magic Show	4.00
	101 Brain Puzzlers	2.50
	Puzzle Me This	3.00
Grosset and Dunlap, Inc. 51 Madison Avenue New York, NY 10010	Great Big Book of Pencil Puzzles	5.00
	Quizzes, Tricks, Stunts, Puzzles, and Brain Teasers from Tell Me Why	5.00
Morrow Quill Paperbacks 105 Madison Avenue New York, NY 10016	The Puzzle Mountain	8.00
Parker Publishing Co. P.O. Box 500 Englewood Cliffs, NJ 07632	Classroom Portfolio of Energizers, Puzzles, Quizzes, Games, and Brain Teasers	12.00
Penguin Books 625 Madison Avenue New York, NY 10022	You Can Do the Cube	2.00
Pinnacle Books, Inc. 1430 Broadway New York, NY 10018	The Simple Solution to the Pyramid	2.00
Pocket Books 1230 Avenue of the Americas New York, NY 10020	Magic Snake Shapes	2.00
	Perplexing Puzzles and Tantalizing Teasers	1.50
Clarkson N. Potter, Inc. One Park Avenue New York, NY 10016	Science Fiction Puzzle Tales	6.50

TABLE 4   BOOKS OF BRAINTEASERS

Publisher	Name	Cost (Approx.)
Prentice-Hall, Inc. Englewood Cliffs, NJ 07632	Mind Tickling Brain Teasers	5.00
	The Simplest Solutions	4.00
	Super Puzzles	5.00
Price/Stern/Sloan Publications, Inc. 410 North La Cienega Boulevard Los Angeles, CA 90048	Solving the Cube	1.00
The Putnam Publishing Group 200 Madison Avenue New York, NY 10016	Creative Growth Games	6.00
	More Creative Growth Games	6.00
Regency Gateway 360 West Superior Street Chicago, IL 60610	The Complete Cube Book	2.50
Schocken Books, Inc. 200 Madison Avenue New York, NY 10016	Brain Games: One Hundred and Thirty-Four Original Scientific Games that Reveal How Your Mind Works	4.00
The Scribner Book Companies, Inc. 597 5th Avenue New York, NY 10017	536 Puzzles and Curious Problems	6.00
	Mathematical Magic	3.50
	One Hundred Games of Logic	8.00
	Science Brain-Twisters, Paradoxes, and Fallacies	4.00
Sterling Publishers Co. 2 Park Avenue New York, NY 10016	Mind Teasers	3.00
Teachers College Press Columbia University 1234 Amsterdam Avenue New York, NY 10027	Math Squared	8.00

SUMMARY

When selected with care, games, brainteasers, and puzzles can be effective in promoting intellectual growth and skills of logical thinking. The selections listed should be useful to teachers and others who receive requests from parents seeking stimulating, inexpensive materials and games to be used with gifted students in the home. Also, gifted children often enjoy designing and formulating the rules of their own games. Playing games, either at home or at school, can provide many hours of challenging experiences and enjoyment for the gifted.

6 Looking to the Future

Hopefully, the current thrust in designing and implementing educational programs for gifted students will become a permanent priority of the American educational system, rather than a passing interest. Unless there is a national commitment to providing appropriate learning experiences for gifted students, the loss caused by undeveloped potential abilities and talents will be serious and irretrievable. Our society will not benefit from the gifts and talents it so desperately needs. There will be a loss to the individual as well. That person who is denied the educational opportunities to develop his or her maximum potential is not only denied a basic right but may have to spend a lifetime in a career or occupation whose demands are far less than the individual is capable of meeting. The goal of providing appropriate educational opportunities for gifted students can be met when all concerned parents and educators and other interested persons unite their efforts and strive to achieve this common objective.

The selection of appropriate learning experiences, teaching methods, and instructional materials for gifted students should be based on the unique needs, interests, and abilities of individual students. They should not be molded to fit a particular program or instructional material. Programs should be designed and materials should be selected to meet the needs of the gifted students they serve.

A major purpose of this book is to provide a central listing of commercially prepared educational materials that have been suggested by various educators concerned with the gifted as being appropriate for these students. Yet, it is not advocated that a program for gifted students should be designed or implemented around the sole use of commercially prepared materials. Many effective materials can be designed by teachers and students. However, a need for a compilation of commercial instructional materials for gifted students has been expressed by educators and parents. The selection and use of any educational material should be based on a careful consideration of students' needs, abilities, learning styles, and interests; the learning and program objectives; and the particular capabilities and instructional styles of teachers.

Many needs continue to exist in the development and effective utilization of commercial materials for gifted students. Relatively few commercially prepared instructional materials have been specifically designed for gifted students. This is especially true in the content areas, such as language arts, mathematics, science, and social studies. In these areas there is a need for the development of materials which utilize and promote the development of thinking skills and higher cognitive processes. The majority of the currently available materials in the content areas merely stress the acquisition of knowledge. The emphasis tends to be on product rather than process.

Instructional materials that employ inquiry, discovery, and/or problem-solving approaches to the study of various content areas could be highly effective with gifted students. The learning process itself, rather than memorization of facts and increasing of knowledge, should be emphasized with gifted students. Science materials that teach the scientific method of research are one example of the types of instructional materials needed.

The lack of field testing of materials with gifted students remains a problem. Field testing of materials and subsequent revisions based on the outcomes would certainly promote the development of materials appropriate for gifted students.

There are still several areas where materials are virtually non-existent. More materials that promote the development of the higher cognitive processes of analysis, synthesis, and evaluation need to be designed. Materials that promote the development of logical thinking skills, critical thinking, and problem solving should also be designed. Many materials produced in these areas are intended for students in the intermediate grades. There is especially a need for thinking skills and problem-solving materials for students in the primary grades and for students at the secondary level. A need also exists in this area for sequentially organized hierarchies of materials.

Instructional materials in career education that are parallel with the interests and abilities of the gifted are presently unavailable. Such materials are definitely needed.

There is a paucity of instructional materials that are expressly designed to teach the processes of group dynamics. Materials designed to facilitate the techniques of debate are lacking. Only a few materials exist that are designed to promote and enhance leadership abilities.

Relatively few instructional aids in futuristic problem solving are obtainable, especially for young students. Primary level materials are also especially needed in science, social studies, and research skills. Although materials designed to promote library research skills are rather widely available, there is a need for materials that emphasize the active involvement of students in the research process, rather than mere knowledge of resources and utilization techniques. Instructional materials that emphasize the scientific method of research are also needed.

Creativity materials for older students are lacking. Materials that promote the combination of creative and logical thinking in problem solving are needed at all age levels. The integration of the affective domain with the cognitive domain in various content areas should be a priority in the development of all educational materials, especially those to be employed in gifted education.

Sequential multilevel materials are also needed in order to allow gifted students to learn at a level commensurate with their ability and to progress at their own rate. Instructional materials that are sequentially organized and appropriate for gifted students are needed in all areas. The majority of currently available instructional aids tend to be rather narrowly focused supplementary materials.

Instructional aids that are to be utilized to foster the development and enhancement of exceptional talents need to be created by qualified persons for both elementary and secondary level students. Appropriate references for the teacher and parent focusing on the development of specialized talents need to be produced.

References and resources for teachers are still needed in many areas. Books pertaining to the development of logical and creative thought processes, the processes of group dynamics and classroom utilization techniques, and the incorporation of futuristic problem solving into the instructional process would assist educators in providing appropriate learning experiences for the gifted. Documents stressing appropriate strategies in identifying and enhancing the leadership capabilities of students who show promise in this area would be valuable contributions to this dimension in the education of our future leaders.

The phenomenal rise in the use of computers has brought about a concomitant need for books that can serve as references for teachers. Since most gifted students spend the majority of their time in school with regular classroom teachers, more resources are needed that allow teachers to more effectively instruct gifted students in the content areas. The scope and sequence of curriculum in the content areas should be addressed in such resources. Books that delineate scope and sequence in areas of instruction included in gifted education programs are also needed.

Since this chapter is concerned with "looking to the future," mention must be made of computers and gifted students. One cannot look very far into the future without being cognizant of the enormous effect computers will have on our lives.

Not without some consternation, the decision was made not to include a listing of software programs that would be appropriate for gifted students. The sheer numerousness of available software programs and the impossibility of examining them all made such a task beyond the scope of this book. To place the magnitude of the problem in perspective, there are now approximately 5,000 different producers of computer software, and approximately 80 percent of these produce educational software! A listing and description of computer hardware would be similarly difficult. The selection of hardware depends on the purposes for which it will be used, and there are numerous possibilities of the utilization of computers with gifted students. Compounding the problem is the fact that there are approximately 350 companies that produce and market computer hardware!

The fact that computer hardware and software are not detailed in this book is by no means intended to de-emphasize the importance of computers with gifted students. There are numerous reasons why computers should be included in the educational programs of gifted students.

Some understanding of computer programming is highly conducive to the development of logical thought processes. Decision making processes are also enhanced. Some degree of computer literacy will be required in many professions in the very near future. This is especially true in those professions that many of today's gifted students can be expected to enter.

Computers can serve as a powerful tool for allowing gifted students to pursue their own interests. The rapidly increasing number of software instructional programs can allow gifted students to pursue higher level studies which might otherwise be unavailable to them. This is especially true in small, rural, and/or somewhat isolated areas, where small schools often cannot provide a variety of advanced courses of study. The possibilities for self-paced learning are also highly beneficial to the educational process for gifted students.

Although many gifted students prefer to write their own programs rather than utilize commercially available software, many software programs, including games programs, can serve to initially acquaint students with computer programs and possibilities. Often the desire to alter a program can prompt a student to pursue a self-study of computer programming and literacy.

The attention sustaining and motivation building aspects of computers are apparent to anyone who has observed students working with computers. These are certainly prime factors in the enhancement of the learning process.

It is wise to carefully consider several factors before purchasing computer hardware. First, define the uses for which the computer hardware is intended. Computer hardware can be used for such a wide variety of purposes, specific systems being more amenable to certain tasks, that it's necessary to define the performance and usage expectations. This should be done even before considering cost variables. Otherwise, the buyer may invest far more in the hardware than is necessary for its purposes. Performance expectations can also enable hardware dealers to make the most cost-effective recommendations for the purchase of hardware.

The types of peripherals (disk drives, cassette recorders, modems, printers, networks, etc.) available and compatible with different hardware systems is another consideration. The costs of these peripherals should be evaluated, as well as the cost of the central processing unit itself.

The number and types of software programs available for the hardware should be examined. There are many more software programs on the market for some computers than for others. Yet the number of programs available is not so important as the types of programs and their compatibility with the tasks for which the computer is to be utilized.

Hardware costs (and the cost of peripherals) must of course be considered. Another consideration is the amount of random access memory and storage on certain computers. Utilization requirements will usually determine the amount of memory needed. Consider not only the amount of random access memory but also the amount of usable memory with a particular unit. The addition of disk drives, for instance, depletes the memory of some computers. The availability of service should also be examined when purchasing hardware.

When making a decision on a software program, it is advisable to see a demonstration of the software first. Descriptions may not always meet expectations. The compatibility of software programs with the hardware you have is a necessary consideration. As with the selection of any materials for gifted students, the compatibility of software with program and individual objectives should be carefully evaluated.

Just as computers are the technological wave of the future, today's gifted students are the human resources in terms of leadership for the future. Therefore, computers combined with education programs for the gifted is a natural alliance.

Appendix A—
Resources in Gifted
Education

Program for the Gifted and Talented
U.S. Department of Education
400 Maryland Avenue
Washington, D.C. 20202

The program specialist responds to communication on matters related to the gifted and talented and disseminates materials on a limited basis.

National/State Leadership Training Institute on the Gifted and Talented
316 West Second Street, Suite 708
Los Angeles, CA 90012

Leadership training through conferences and publications is the primary aim. A catalog of publications is available upon request.

The Educational Resources Information Clearinghouse on Handicapped and Gifted
The Council for Exceptional Children
1920 Association Drive
Reston, VA 22091

The National Clearinghouse for the Gifted and Talented serves as the central clearinghouse for all information pertaining to the gifted, talented, and creative.

Creative Education Foundation
State University College at Buffalo
1300 Elmwood Avenue
Buffalo, NY 14222

Workshops and publications focusing on creativity at all age levels are provided through the foundation. *The Journal of Creative Behavior* is published quarterly under their auspices.

National Merit Scholarship Corporation
One American Plaza
Evanston, IL 60201

The national merit scholarship program is an independently financed competition for college undergraduate scholarships. Two major purposes are the basis for this program: to promote academic excellence by focusing attention on the intellectually talented and to encourage corporations, businesses, foundations, and other organizations to provide scholarships.

NATIONAL AND INTERNATIONAL ORGANIZATIONS

The American Association for the Gifted
15 Gramercy Park
New York, NY 10003

The association strives to seek cooperation with other agencies and organizations to foster programs for the gifted and talented, specifically in the arts and humanities.

American Mensa, Ltd.
1701 West Third Street
Brooklyn, NY 11223

The organization is composed of members who score in the ninety-eighth percentile or above on an intelligence test. Meetings, research, and a journal are the major endeavors of this international group.

Association for Gifted and Talented Students
1627 Frankfort Street
New Orleans, LA 70122

A national organization open to educators, parents, and others interested in gifted and talented students. A newsletter and conferences are a major thrust of this association.

The Association for the Gifted (TAG)
The Council for Exceptional Children
1920 Association Drive
Reston, VA 22091

One of the twelve divisions of the Council for Exceptional Children, the Association for the Gifted sponsors many projects for the membership which consists of parents and professionals. Activities include a quarterly journal, *The Journal for the Education of the Gifted,* a newsletter, and bonus publications. Regional and national conferences are conducted and affiliate state organizations expand the scope of the association to the state and local levels.

The Council of State Directors of Programs for Gifted
George Fichter, Consultant
Programs for Gifted/Talented
Division of Special Education
933 High Street
Workington, OH 43085

The membership of the council is limited to persons responsible for gifted education in each state department of education. The council undertakes surveys and disseminates information.

Gifted Child Society, Inc.
59 Glen Gray Road
Oakland, NJ 07436

The organization primarily sponsors out-of-school enrichment classes for gifted students in New Jersey. Other endeavors have focused on establishing a national network of parent organizations interested in the gifted and talented.

Gifted Students Institute for Research and Development
611 Ryan Plaza Drive
Suite 1149
Arlington, TX 76011

The institute conducts summer programs in several locations for gifted upper elementary and junior and senior high school students. Other objectives include conducting research and providing consultative services to schools and agencies wanting to serve the gifted.

Mensa Gifted Children Program
4817 W. Kirk
Skokie, IL 60077

This organization, which acts as a support group for gifted students through information dissemination and conferences and seminars, is a function of American Mensa.

The National Association for Creative Children and Adults
8080 Spring Valley Drive
Cincinnati, OH 45236

The association publishes *The Creative Child and Adult Quarterly* and is interested in better understanding and application of research on creativity.

National Association for Gifted Children
5100 North Edgewood Drive
St. Paul, MN 55112

Open to professionals and parents, the association publishes the *Gifted Child Quarterly,* a newsletter and conducts meetings at the local, state, and national levels.

World Council for Gifted and Talented Children, Inc.
University of South Florida
Human Services, Room 412
Tampa, FL 33620

This international organization sponsors the World Congress on the Gifted, publishes *Gifted International,* and a newsletter.

JOURNALS AND MAGAZINES

Challenge
Box 299
Carthage, IL 62321-0299

Published five times a year, this publication presents practical information for teachers and parents of gifted students.

Chart Your Own Course
G/C/T Publishing Company
Box 66707
Mobile, AL 36660

A magazine for gifted, creative, and talented students, with many of the articles, puzzles, games, poems, etc., written by them. It is published four times a year.

The Creative Child and Adult Quarterly
The National Association for Creative Children and Adults
8080 Spring Valley Drive
Cincinnati, OH 45236

Research and practical application of creativity in psychology and education are the central focus of this quarterly journal.

The Gifted Child Quarterly
The National Association for Gifted Children
5100 North Edgewood Drive
St. Paul, MN 55112

The journal for professionals and parents contains research and practical suggestions on the gifted and talented students.

Gifted/Creative/Talented Children
G/C/T Publishing Company
Box 66654
Mobile, AL 36606

The magazine, published five times a year, contains a variety of articles for parents and teachers.

Gifted Children Newsletter
Gifted and Talented Publications, Inc.
P.O. Box 115
Sewell, NJ 08080

The newsletter for parents of gifted students contains a wide range of information, including books, toys, and games appropriate for the gifted.

Gifted International
The World Council for Gifted and Talented Children, Inc.
University of South Florida
Human Services, Room 412
Tampa, FL 33620

Published semiannually by the World Council for Gifted and Talented Children, the focus of this journal is current research at the international level.

The Journal for the Education of the Gifted
The Association for the Gifted
1920 Association Drive
Reston, VA 22091

Issued quarterly and directed to professionals and parents, the journal covers major topics such as research, innovative programming, reviews of literature, and historical perspectives.

The Journal of Creative Behavior
Creative Education Foundation
State University College at Buffalo
1300 Elmwood Avenue
Buffalo, NY 14222

This quarterly journal, published by the Creative Education Foundation, emphasizes teaching and research in the areas of creativity and problem solving at all age levels.

Roeper Review: A Journal on Gifted Child Education
Roeper City and Country School
2190 North Woodward
Bloomfield Hills, MI 48013

This journal is published four times a year and stresses practical application of gifted education in the classroom. Humanistic and global points of view are presented.

COMPETITIONS

Arts Recognition and Talent Search
Box 2876
Princeton, NJ 08541

Developed by the Educational Testing Service and an activity of the National Foundation for Advancement in the Arts, this national program seeks to identify, recognize, and encourage high school seniors outstanding in music, theatre, dance, writing, and visual arts.

Commission on Presidential Scholars
U.S. Department of Education
400 Maryland Avenue S.W.
Washington, D.C. 20202

Through the Commission, students, outstanding intellectually as determined by their high scores on a national examination, are given national recognition.

Future Problem Solving Program
Coe College
Cedar Rapids, IA 52402

A national competition focused on future problems to be solved by gifted students from grades four through twelve. New topics are selected annually and a variety of publications, including a newsletter, are available.

National Academic Games Program
P.O. Box 214
Newhall, CA 91322

The national games are held annually for elementary, middle school, and senior high school students. The topics include social studies, mathematics, language arts, and logic.

Olympics of the Mind
Creative Competitions
P.O. Box 27
Glassboro, NJ 08028

Teams of students from kindergarten to grade twelve compete to determine solutions to a variety of problems. A newsletter and other publications are available to entering schools.

Appendix B

Your assistance is solicited to further the search for commercially prepared materials, professional references, games, brainteasers, and puzzles. The form provided is for your convenience and can be photocopied to be shared with others. Although the authors would like to know the contributors, it is not necessary to complete the personal section of the information sheet. Thank you.

Return to: Dr. Frances Karnes; Dr. Emily Collins
            Box 8207 Southern Station
            University of Southern Mississippi
            Hattiesburg, MS 39401

SUGGESTION FORM

The following commercially prepared materials are suggested for use with the gifted:

Material/Publisher	Suggested Level	Approximate Cost (if known)

The following professional references are suggested:

Publication **Publisher**

_____

_____

_____

_____

The following games, brainteasers, and puzzles are suggested for gifted students:

Game/Brainteaser/Puzzle **Distributor/Publisher** **Address (if known)**

_____

_____

_____

_____

NAME: _____
        First   Middle   Last

ADDRESS: _____
           Street   City   State   ZIP

____ Administrator   ____ Teacher Educator

____ Counselor   ____ Teacher/Regular

____ Local Director   ____ Teacher/Specialized

____ Parent   ____ State Consultant

____ Other _____